# PREFACE

For some thirty-five years now I have been writing on the three-year Sunday and festal lectionary. My aim has been to help homilists mine the treasures of the Scriptures and to enable the faithful to derive profit from the liturgical readings. This present work is a more modest attempt to comment on the biblical background of the twenty mysteries of the rosary and to recommend how one may use them for prayer and meditation. The Word of God thus becomes the raw material for reflection and action.

I am indebted to those who encouraged me to undertake this task. In particular, I wish to thank my wife, Barbara Lynne, for reading the entire manuscript and making many helpful suggestions.

I dedicate this book to Rosi and Don Hallam, my sister-in-law and brother-in-law. They have taught me through actions what this little work tries to express in words. My indebtedness to them is incalculable.

*Feast of the Visitation, May 31, 2008*
*John F. Craghan*

# TABLE OF CONTENTS

# INTRODUCTION

## The Nature of Prayer

What happens when we engage in prayer? What really takes place when we resolve to banish our everyday distractions and seek to encounter our God in prayer? What are the challenges and opportunities involved in this exercise of communion with our God? What follows is not a detailed response to such questions. Rather, it is an attempt to underline some of the dimensions and aspects of prayer.

In our society the media constantly bombards us on all sides, not only with daily events, but also with their presumed meanings or interpretations. Genuine prayer compels us to react to this barrage of news. It forces us to ask about God's viewpoint on reality. Prayer challenges us to dare to uncover how God would assess the news and how God wishes us to respond. Our liturgical prayer of the faithful is at least one way in which we organize our answer.

Abraham Heschel, the distinguished Jewish scholar, adroitly explains the difference between language and prayer. He unequivocally states that while the purpose of language is to inform, the purpose of prayer is to partake. To a certain degree, prayer is the call to withdraw for a while from the cacophony of daily life and to search for both time and space to commune with this God. In such time and space, we are to reassess our priorities in the light of this God's will and plan for us. Prayer gives us the opportunity to rub up against this God and attempt to see things from a wholly other perspective.

Prayer enables us to be genuinely human. It removes us from the centripetal force of egoism and energizes us with the centrifugal power of union with God. One may go so far as to say that a life without prayer is not a genuinely human life. We can only react to our ordinary life with its multiple contacts by including contact with the One whose relationship gives value and worth to all our other relationships. To pray is to admit that we are all too human, that we are beings residing in a fragile world who need the One who provides order and purpose for us and our cosmos.

Prayer is a many-splendored reality. We pray in times of normalcy (orientation) when we suffer no great shocks and can easily break out into praise of our God's ongoing goodness and relentless providence. We pray in times of despair and disaster (disorientation) when our whole world comes crashing down. We experience the death of a loved one, the vulnerability of the human body, and the vicissitudes of human relationships. We pray in times of new life and amazement (reorientation) when we encounter a God of surprises, a God who puts a new song in our hearts when Good Friday afternoon gives way to Easter Sunday morning.

Prayer is a communal exercise because it is grounded in

covenant, i.e., a relationship in which God, the community, and the individual are integral partners. At prayer we make the problems and concerns of others our own problems and concerns. The cry of our sisters and brothers—"Why have you forsaken me?"—must trigger our response. In prayer, both the pain and the joy of countless others become our pain and joy. As Saint Paul expresses it, "If one member suffers, all suffer together with it; if one member is honored, all rejoice together with it" (1 Corinthians 12:26). Prayer is never an ego trip.

Our model of prayer is Jesus in the Gospel of Luke. At his baptism, when choosing the Twelve, during Peter's confession, his own transfiguration, the moment prior to giving the Our Father, through his agony in the garden, and while suffering on the cross, Jesus is at prayer. More than the other evangelists, Luke is ever intent to emphasize the absolute necessity of prayer for his gentile-Christian audience that knows nothing of the prayer of petition. The Jesus of Luke's Gospel feels compelled to undertake long seasons of prayer as he plots his ministry. It is hardly surprising that this gospel opens with the prayer of devout Jews in the Temple and closes with the prayer of the disciples in the same place following Jesus' ascension.

## The Meaning of Mystery

Whenever we hear the word "mystery," we think almost instinctively of something that is beyond our ken, something that is esoteric and utterly impenetrable. However, the biblical background, while it does not eliminate the element of something secret or hidden, suggests a much more positive understanding. In that setting we are ushered into the presence of God, who communicates to us (often through a prophet or spokesperson) some aspect of the plan of salvation.

In the prophetic literature, God is depicted as being surrounded by a heavenly council that makes decisions and recommendations. Prophets are seen as either members of such a council or as eavesdropping on the final decisions of the council. In the Book of Amos, for example, God undertakes nothing without first revealing the heavenly plan to his servants, the prophets (3:7). In his attack on the false prophets, Jeremiah poses this question: "For who has stood in the council of the Lord so as to see and to hear his word?" (23:18). If such false prophets had really stood in the divine council and proclaimed God's message to the people, they would have brought such people back from their evil ways (Jeremiah 23:22).

Later Jewish literature shows a development in such communications as God reveals a variety of matters to humans, frequently in highly symbolic language. In the Book of Daniel, "mystery" is the revelation that King Nebuchadnezzar received in a dream about the large statue and one that Daniel must uncover. "Then the mystery was revealed to Daniel in a vision..." (2:19). In a later episode Nebuchadnezzar experiences another terrifying dream and, when his own experts prove unsuccessful in interpreting it, turns to Daniel: "I know that you are endowed with a holy, divine spirit and that no mystery is too difficult for you. Hear the dream that I saw; tell me its interpretation" (4:9).

Such usage provides the background for grasping the notion of "mystery" in the New Testament. As used in Paul and elsewhere, mystery is basically a new revelation about God's plan of salvation. What was hidden in God for such long periods of time is now revealed. In First Corinthians, God's mystery is fundamentally Jesus Christ crucified. The plan that God conceived and that lay hidden in him from the start is now realized in Jesus Christ. Paul views himself as a steward who shares this mystery with his communities. The author of Colossians understands the mystery of Christ to be nothing less than the divine plan for humankind's salvation that, having been kept secret in the past, is now revealed to Christians. At the same time, in employing the term "mystery," Paul is fully aware that it is never grasped by merely ordinary means of communication, but only by faith. Hence a dimension of obscurity remains in the human participation in God's disclosure.

Such an understanding of mystery provides no little help as we discuss the mysteries of the rosary. While we gain insight into the meaning of the biblical texts and discover God's plan in a variety of events, we still experience a state of awe, a feeling of being overwhelmed at not being able to see with perfect clarity. As Pope Paul VI puts it, a mystery is a reality imbued with the hidden presence of God. While we encounter the divine presence, we realize all too well that we cannot penetrate the totality reality. Perhaps such an experience is not unlike human love. As love for another grows, we feel we are incapable of expressing that love in simple propositions. We conclude that we must make room for mystery.

## The Rosary and the Scriptures

With two exceptions (the assumption and the coronation of Mary) the mysteries of the rosary are intended to be reflections on specific biblical texts. Thus the Word of God is intended to interact with our efforts at prayer. "Indeed, the word of God is living and active, sharper than any two-edged sword, piercing until it divides soul from spirit, joints from marrow; it is able to judge the thoughts and intentions of the heart" (Hebrews 4:12). Our task, therefore, is to allow the Word to enter our entire being, to permeate our whole person in such a way that it can console and challenge us, that it can surprise and reenergize us. The Word of God is not meant to be a dusty collection of obscure texts from the ancient Near East, but a dynamic series of encounters between God and humans. Hearing the Word of God always demands a response, whether that response be praise, adoration, petition, confession, or awe. If we truly hear the Word, we begin to sense its power and its efficacy. "So shall my word be that goes out from my mouth; it shall not return to me empty, but it shall accomplish that which I purpose, and succeed in the thing for which I sent it" (Isaiah 55:11).

Borrowing a phrase from Pope Pius XII, Pope Paul VI

in his apostolic exhortation (*Marialis Cultus*, 1974) calls the rosary the compendium of the entire gospel. In 2002, Pope John Paul II enhanced this compendium when he added the luminous mysteries (the mysteries of light) to the recitation of the rosary. In addition to the joyful, sorrowful, and glorious mysteries, we enlarge our focus by reflecting on the following: the baptism of Jesus in the Jordan, the wedding feast at Cana, the proclamation of the kingdom, the transfiguration, and the institution of the Eucharist. These luminous mysteries clearly complement the others. At the same time, they draw our attention to other facets of the Good News that offer both challenge and hope. As a result, the rosary as the epitome of the entire gospel is intensified by including events from the public ministry of Jesus. As the gospel focus is enlarged, the opportunities for prayer increase.

## Christological Emphasis

While the principal component of the rosary is the Hail Mary, we are not to think that this traditional prayer disregards or minimizes in any way the person and mission of Jesus (Christology). When we consider these twenty mysteries in their totality, they are Christ-oriented and Christ-centered. The Church, therefore, urges us to appreciate the total plan of salvation that attains its zenith in the work and achievement of Jesus. Such an orientation is in keeping with the thrust of the liturgy as a whole. While the feasts of Mary and other saints enjoy a fitting place in the Church's public worship, according to the Second Vatican Council's constitution on the liturgy, the minds of the faithful are to be focused primarily on the feasts of the Lord in which the unfolding of the plan of salvation is celebrated in the course of the year.

To be sure, Mary, like us, is also redeemed. As a consequence, she is in solidarity with all humans in their need for salvation and cares for all the sisters and brothers of her Son in their journey of faith. In underlining the central place of Jesus in the rosary, the Church also acknowledges that Mary occupies a conspicuous place in the plan of salvation. The Church recognizes that she is a model who encapsulates the desires and hopes of all the faithful. By situating Mary within the larger frame of salvation, we recognize that she is only fully understood and appreciated, not in the splendid isolation of her privileges, but in her response to the Word of God. We call her blessed because she hears that Word and acts upon it.

## How to Pray the Rosary With Scripture

This book adopts the following order in approaching the mysteries of the rosary: The Joyful Mysteries (Chapter One), the Luminous Mysteries (Chapter Two), the Sorrowful Mysteries (Chapter Three), and the Glorious Mysteries (Chapter Four). It moves from the Lukan infancy narrative and the public ministry of Jesus through the passion and death to the exaltation of Jesus, concluding with Mary's assumption and coronation. With the exception of the last two glorious mysteries, this order follows the outline of the biblical texts themselves. As such, the rosary is indeed a compendium of the entire Good News of Jesus.

Each mystery begins with a *focus*. This attempts to orient our thoughts to some particular aspects of the mystery to be considered. It may simply challenge our everyday reactions and attitudes to biblical scenes, for example, the clash of wills in the agony in the garden or our state of amazement at Jesus' cryptic question in the finding in the Temple. To some degree, the focus resembles the practice in certain religious communities of providing points or material for the following morning's meditation. It channels and directs our attention to some salient dimension of the biblical text. To that extent, the focus seeks to grip our attention by underlining certain facets of a given biblical passage.

After the focus, there is a reference to the *biblical text* or *texts* to be read. The reader is encouraged to read the designated passages slowly and prayerfully from a viable modern translation. This recommendation is based on the fact that there is no substitute for knowing what the text actually says. The focus mentioned above should guide the reading of each text.

Following the biblical text reference is a *textual explanation*. This explanation will vary in length depending on the number and density of the passages. It seeks to employ the best of modern biblical scholarship in ferreting out the levels of meaning in the texts. Part of that sound biblical scholarship is the modified two-source theory for the first three gospels. Matthew, Mark, and Luke are known as the Synoptic Gospels since they share a common viewpoint, one quite distinct from the Gospel of John. The two sources in question are Mark (the first written gospel) and Q (principally a collection of Jesus' sayings, for example, the Our Father). Matthew and Luke make independent use of Mark and Q. This is a modified two-source theory insofar as Matthew and Luke also employ their own special sources, for example, the Magi in Matthew 2:1–12 and the shepherds in Luke 2:8–20. The modifications of Matthew and Luke provide an invaluable key for uncovering their special interests and emphases. Sound biblical scholarship and a richer experience of prayer, therefore, can go hand in glove.

The last element in the format consists of *reflections*. This represents an effort to disengage from the biblical texts' themes, points, or aspects that may impact our recitation of the rosary and our way of experiencing a particular mystery. The riches of the Bible are inestimable, offering us seemingly endless resources for both prayer and action.

It is not recommended that the reader go through all five mysteries in a chapter. Rather, it may be more rewarding to concentrate on only one mystery at a time. For example, read only the material on the annunciation when reciting the joyful mysteries, leaving the rest of the chapter for other prayer times. The suggested strategy is to divide and conquer.

# CHAPTER ONE

# THE JOYFUL MYSTERIES

## The Annunciation

**FOCUS:** Our God calls us to accept his will in everyday circumstances. But how are we to react when confronted by that plan? Given our particular vocation in life, we may run the risk of doubting our God's capacity to see us through those very difficult moments. All too often we suffer from a collision of wills, that is, God's and our own. We are challenged to accept God's plan, even though we do not see all its specifics. To accept or not to accept—that is the question. Do we dare to be open to what God asks?

**TEXT:** Luke 1:5–38

**TEXTUAL EXPLANATION:** Unlike Matthew, Luke chooses to focus on Mary, not Joseph, in the first two chapters of his gospel. As we will see, he will present Mary, not simply as a disciple, but indeed as the model disciple. We have no indication that Mary herself was one of the sources for Luke's portrait of the mother of Jesus. Thus he does not provide us with personal reminiscences of Mary. Rather, he uses his sources in such a way as to show his readership how one should respond to God's Word.

In contrast to Matthew (1:18–25), Luke has two annunciation of birth accounts, one to Zechariah (1:5–25) and another to Mary (1:26–38). Luke is offering his readers a diptych, a two-panel piece in which one panel is used to interpret the other. In the first panel, Zechariah hears the incredible news that his wife Elizabeth and he are finally going to have a son: "Your wife Elizabeth will bear you a son, and you will name him John" (1:13). Zechariah responds to Gabriel's message with a question: "How will I know that this is so? For I am an old man, and my wife is getting on in years" (1:18). The outcome of the scene is that Zechariah is mute, unable to speak. Gabriel then explains the reason for this punishment: "…because you did not believe my words, which will be fulfilled in their time" (1:20).

The contrast with Mary could not be more striking. Mary is called "favored one" and is bidden not to fear for she has found favor with God (1:28–30). She will bear a son who possesses a twofold identity; he will be both Son of God and Son of David (1:31–33). The message is a bewildering one for Mary since she is only betrothed or engaged, and the final marriage ceremony that would permit living with Joseph has not yet taken place. As a result, Mary poses a question: "How can this be, since I am a virgin?" (1:34). Gabriel responds that all this is the working of the Holy Spirit. This Spirit will come upon her and the child to be born will be called holy. The power of the Most High will overshadow her, and hence her son will be called Son of God (1:35). After receiving a sign (Elizabeth's pregnancy), Mary, Luke's quintessential disciple, replies: "Here am I, the servant of the Lord" (1:38). The contrast with Zechariah is all too obvious.

What Luke has done is to put the basic Christian confession of faith on Gabriel's lips: Jesus is Son of God and Son of David (Romans 1:3–4). Luke's true estimate of Mary becomes evident in her reaction to this confession of faith as the servant of the Lord. For Luke, Mary is thus the first to hear the Good News and respond in faith.

REFLECTIONS: With whom can we identify? The gospels frequently challenge us with various casts of biblical characters. For example, in Mark, will we identify with Jesus' male disciples in the garden who abandon Jesus and flee or with the women disciples of Jesus who are present on Golgotha, looking on from a distance? In Luke's annunciation scenes, with whom can we identify? Too often, it seems, we have played the role of Zechariah by being unable or unwilling to admit that God can achieve the seemingly impossible. All too frequently, we cannot begin to imagine that our God has the capacity to surprise us. On the other hand, do we dare to open ourselves in faith and accept what appears to defy logic and good common sense? We must candidly acknowledge that Mary, in this Lukan scene, is indeed a hard act to follow.

We noted in the introduction that in its biblical usage,

"mystery" has to do with the revelation of God's plan. Such usage may well give us pause. God's plan of salvation does not involve only a chosen few—it embraces all of us. Especially through our vocation in life, we are partners with our God and our community in this plan. This scene of the annunciation to Mary poses questions such as the following: How well or how poorly do we react to God's plan or will in the demanding setting of daily life? How well or how poorly do we envision our vocation as the means to enhance and improve the situations of those who depend on us? The annunciation of Mary is a scene that is played over and over again in that series of challenging duties that comprise our everyday existence.

We also observed in the introduction that "mystery" as the disclosure of God's plan does not remove all elements of obscurity. As Paul remarks, we see indistinctly now (1 Corinthians 13:12). However, it is comforting to note that Mary also had to deal with less than clear pictures of God's plan. As we will see in Luke 2:19, 51, Mary has to ponder and reflect on the meaning of the events in the life of Jesus. She lives not only a life of faith but also one of hope—a hope that will be ultimately realized in Jesus' exaltation. With this Lukan Mary, we are surely in good company.

## The Visitation

FOCUS: What is our understanding of faith? Often it may be limited to a list of articles or propositions to which we assent. While that is an element of faith, it is not the total package. First and foremost, faith is the acceptance of a person. As we say in the Creed, we believe *in* one God. This implies that we ground ourselves in a God who reveals himself to us. It is also the case with faith in humans. Thus I believe in you, I believe you, and I am prepared to believe what you tell me. It is this personal dimension of Mary's faith that Luke will highlight in the visitation scene.

Immediately upon hearing Elizabeth's beatitude about her faith, Mary breaks out into praise of God for all that has transpired. Perhaps it is this capacity to praise that may pique our attention—not simply praise of God, but also praise of others for what they have accomplished.

TEXT: Luke 1:39–56

TEXTUAL EXPLANATION: The Spirit is extremely active in this scene. The child in Elizabeth's womb (John the Baptist) is filled with that Spirit (1:15) and causes his mother to recognize the Messiah in Mary's womb. The result is that Elizabeth is also filled with the Spirit, just as her husband Zechariah will be (1:67). In this condition, Elizabeth pronounces a blessing on Mary, but more so on the child of her womb (1:42). Such a blessing has Old Testament roots. Deborah praises Jael as "most blessed of women" (Judges 5:24) for her part in fulfilling God's saving plan. "Blessed shall be the fruit of your womb" (Deuteronomy 28:4) is also a blessing pronounced by Moses for obedience to the covenant.

Luke has shaped this scene by using one of his unique

traditions: the saying of the woman in the crowd (11:27–28). Elizabeth's praise of Mary ("…blessed is the fruit of your womb" [1:42]) matches the saying of the woman in the crowd ("Blessed is the womb that bore you…" [11:27]). Mary is thus the object of praise because of her child. However, Elizabeth's beatitude ("And blessed is she who believed…" [1:45]) corresponds to Jesus' reaction to the woman in the crowd ("Blessed rather are those who hear the word of God and obey it" [11:28]). Luke's comment, therefore, is that Mary is the great believer in that she completely opens herself to God and his plan. Again Luke offers the faith response of Mary as a decided contrast to the unbelieving Zechariah.

The Magnificat is a psalm of declarative praise (one that praises God for something specific and concrete) that Luke places on Mary's lips. It is a mosaic of Old Testament passages that comment on the coming of Jesus. It is greatly influenced by the canticle of Hannah after the miraculous birth of her son Samuel (1 Samuel 2:1–10). The introduction expresses Mary's overwhelming joy (Luke 1:46–47). Verses 48–50 offer motives for praising God, such as the overcoming of her lowliness (Mary's virginity is tantamount to the barrenness of the Old Testament women like Sarah, Rebekah, Rachel, and Hannah) and the Exodus-like accomplishments ("great things," see Deuteronomy 10:21). Verses 51 and 52 anticipate the victory achieved through Jesus' death and resurrection, the time when God's arm will be manifested and Jesus will be exalted to God's right hand (Acts 2:33). Verse 53 contains reversal strategy ("hungry…

rich"). Finally, in verse 55, God has acted according to the promises and blessings to Abraham and his descendants (see Genesis 12:2–3; 18:18; 22:17–18).

REFLECTIONS: There is a movement in Elizabeth's address to Mary that must command our attention. In Luke 1:42, Elizabeth blesses or praises Mary because of the child she has conceived. Thus the praise is directed toward Jesus. In verse 45, however, she articulates not a blessing, but a beatitude about Mary: "Blessed are you who believed that what was spoken to you by the Lord would be fulfilled." In this case it is Mary's faith, not the conception of Jesus, that Luke highlights.

Faith is, first and foremost, the acceptance of a person. I believe in you; I believe you. Thus Mary grounds her entire being in the person of her God. What follows next is the acceptance of God's command or mission. It is such faith that we are urged to emulate. While we are not to denigrate propositions or doctrines, we must first accept the person of God who chooses to share the plan of salvation with us. It is this openness to the person of God that Mary demonstrates in such a compelling way in this scene. The contrast with Elizabeth's husband is once again evident.

In the Magnificat, Mary breaks forth in exuberant praise of God—something that Zechariah will also do in the Benedictus (Luke 1:67–79). It is the ability to free oneself from the shackles of egoism, to move beyond one's focus on self that Mary demonstrates in the visitation. What God has done for her and what God will do for others in the ministry, passion, death, and resurrection of Jesus now advances center stage.

It is this note of praise that speaks to us today, but perhaps in a different way. While we may not find it too bothersome to praise God and laud the "great things," we may find it much more difficult and even distasteful to praise our fellow humans and their accomplishments. It is indeed a tragedy that we must wait for the moment of death to acknowledge the goodness and generosity of others. In our battle against the insidious forces of ego, we are urged to repeat the hymn of creation when we observe the achievements of others: "It is good, very good!"

## The Nativity

FOCUS: Peace, manger, inn—these are three powerful symbols that rivet our attention at Christmas. The mention of Caesar Augustus evokes the dimension of world peace. However, as we recall Luke's account of the birth, we may have to widen our horizons. If charity begins at home, why not peace? Domestic peace and world peace seem to be intrinsically related. The symbol of the manger usually brings to mind the utter poverty of the family in that they are forced to celebrate the birth in such dismal surroundings. Finally there is the symbol of the inn. We usually conjure up images of inhospitable Bethlehem innkeepers who slam the doors of their establishments and the doors of their hearts in the face of the pregnant woman and her husband. But is Luke intimating something much more profound than lack of accommodations in the inn symbol? Is there not a more positive reality to "no room in the inn"?

TEXT: Luke 2:1–20

TEXTUAL EXPLANATION: The manger probably refers to Isaiah 1:3 where the Greek Old Testament says that the donkey knows the manger of its lord. The inn may allude to Jeremiah 14:8 where only the passing traveler spends the night and then moves on. The swaddling may call to mind Wisdom 7:4–5, where the great King Solomon is swaddled. By presenting Jesus as lying in a manger, Luke suggests the place where God provides for his people and is recognized by them. By not staying in an inn and then moving on, Jesus is now understood to be permanently present to his people. Finally, the swaddling announces the royal dignity of Jesus.

Luke introduces the shepherds because of their association with Bethlehem (see Genesis 35:9–12; Micah 4:8; 5:2). Using a text such as Isaiah 9:5–6, Luke has the shepherds announce the message of the angel: that a Messiah, son of David, has been born who is also Savior and Lord. The reality of the resurrection and exaltation is already present in the conception and birth of Jesus. There next follows a theophany, a manifestation of God ("the heavenly host"). The angels recognize in the beginning what the disciples will later come to learn, that is, the presence of the Messiah King.

In Luke 2:15, the shepherds decide to verify the message of the angel. By seeing the baby lying in the manger (an allusion to Isaiah 1:3), the shepherds represent the Israel that recognizes the manger as the place where God provides for his people. Luke adds two reactions: (1) that of the shepherds and (2) that of the audience ("all who heard it"). The shepherds react by understanding the angel's message about the child. When they subsequently return, they break out into praise of God. They thereby anticipate those generations of believers who will also glorify the Lord for what they have heard and seen. The audience reacts by being astonished.

Among all those astonished in this infancy narrative (see Luke 1:63), only Mary is described as treasuring and pondering these events. Mary's reaction is all the more telling since Mary is the only witness in the infancy account who reappears in the ministry of Jesus. Mary's pondering concerns the God-given interpretation of unclear revelation. As the model disciple of Jesus, she will correctly interpret the events only after Jesus' glorification. For the present, however, she must still ponder the mystery of her child.

**REFLECTIONS:** The notion of peace is a significant element in Luke's account of the Nativity. The canticle of the heavenly host concludes thus: "...on earth peace among those whom God favors" (2:14). The peace accruing from this singular event is destined for those whom God favors with his grace. It is not by accident that Luke links this peace with his earlier mention of Caesar Augustus (2:1). The very mention of his name would alert Luke's audience to peace as Augustus' great claim to fame. In 29 BC he ushered in a new era of peace by terminating almost a century of civil war. This age of Augustan peace became the object of widespread propaganda that impacted Luke's readers. For them Augustus was known as the savior of the whole world. One inscription hailed his birthday as the start of good news for the world.

At prayer we must envision ourselves not only as recipients of peace, but also as its promoters. While we may argue that we cannot easily influence world peace, we know that we can certainly impact domestic peace. Luke's account of the Nativity is the clarion call to reconciliation. We are asked to eliminate all those barriers that keep us apart from each other. We are challenged to remove all those obstacles that prevent truly human communication. To forgive past wrongs and to seek forgiveness for past offenses is nothing less than the prayerful celebration of the Nativity.

Luke is patently intent upon emphasizing the role of the manger by mentioning it no less than three times (2:7, 12, 16). Usually we understand the manger as an obvious sign of the family's poverty. We also picture the inn as that wretched place of gross inhospitality. Luke, however, may very likely be appealing to the Scriptures. In the Greek Old Testament text of Isaiah 1:3, the donkey knows the manger of its lord, but Israel does not recognize *its* Lord. However, through the shepherds, Luke proclaims that Israel does indeed recognize the presence of its Lord in Jesus. Similarly the inn is probably linked to Jeremiah 14:8 where the Lord, the hope of Israel, is accused of being like the overnight salesperson who flits from one lodging to another. For Luke, God is now permanently present to Israel in Jesus, who rejects the inn in favor of ongoing residence.

These images of the God who provides must evoke a reaction. This God who meets the needs of the people must provoke us to similar action. The sharing of our gifts should not be limited to one day in December. Christmas is that ongoing reality in which we recognize our God in others by addressing their concerns. The manger and the inn can thus become powerful symbols of human care and provision. Luke invites us to dwell on these symbols, and through prayer, convert them into dynamos of ceaseless activity.

## The Presentation

FOCUS: This scene raises at least two issues: (1) our service to others by revealing the message of Jesus and (2) our endurance of pain. Luke will have Simeon speak of Jesus as a light for revelation to the gentiles. We are not only the recipients of that light, but also its bearers. This passage challenges us to take our place in the long line of those who witness to Jesus. The second issue, our coping with pain, places us in the company of Mary. She must endure the tragedy of her son's crucifixion. This must pose the following question for us: Do we see pain and suffering as something to be stoically endured or the raw material for growth?

TEXT: Luke 2:22–40

TEXTUAL EXPLANATION: In composing this episode, Luke has drawn on the story of Elkanah and Hannah in 1 Samuel 1—2. After the barren Hannah finally gives birth to a son (Samuel), the couple proceeds to the shrine at Shiloh to offer their son to the Lord. There the aged priest, Eli, accepts the dedication of their son to God's service.

Although only the purification (Leviticus 12:1–8) required going to the sanctuary, Luke mentions the redemption of the firstborn male (see Exodus 13:2, 12, 15), since this leads to the meeting with the latter-day Eli (Simeon) who confronts the latter-day Elkanah and Hannah (Joseph and Mary). Luke indicates the greatness of Jesus by dwelling on the Jewish law, the prophetic spirit, and the Temple cult. In the Canticle of Simeon ("…now you are dismissing your servant in peace…" [2:29]), Luke anticipates his second volume, the Acts of the Apostles, where the message of Jesus will be "a light for revelation to the gentiles" (2:32). In his second oracle (2:34–35), Luke has Simeon anticipate the Jewish rejection of Jesus during the ministry and the passion. In this process of discrimination (the sword), Mary will experience pain as Israel as a whole fails to respond.

In Anna the prophetess (together with Simeon), Luke probably refers to the gift of the Spirit at Pentecost. Here Anna represents the devout, the so-called "Poor Ones of Israel." In verse 40 ("The child grew and became strong, filled with wisdom; and the favor of God was upon him"),

Luke has Samuel's growth and development in mind (1 Samuel 2:21, 26). The reader is thus prepared for the moment when Jesus will appear in the synagogue in Nazareth (Luke 4:16).

**REFLECTIONS:** In Luke's account, Mary will experience pain and sorrow at the people's rejection of Jesus. She will also endure the sword of discrimination. This conjures up the sword of judgment that destroys some and spares others (see Ezekial 14:17). Mary too must embrace the harsh demands of discipleship. By consistently accepting such demands, she enjoys a preeminent place in the family of disciples.

At prayer we are bidden to see the pain and suffering in our own lives as linked to the demands of discipleship. We are asked to see them, not as extraneous, meaningless events, but as the essential ingredients for our journey with Jesus and with one another. They are our building blocks for growth, our sword of discrimination leading to Christian maturity. By coping daily with these upsetting occurrences, we share the company of no less a person than the mother of Jesus.

We have no problem in accepting Jesus as the light of revelation to the gentiles. But do we see ourselves in this capacity as well? At our baptism, we received the light of Christ symbolized by the lit candle and were commissioned to be his prophets or spokespersons. The world at large is now our congregation, and we are asked to share that light with all those with whom we come into contact. These need not be moments of grandiose proclamation. More often than not, they are the times when we exhibit patience with others and offer them consolation by our words and actions. To borrow a well-known phrase, the torch has been passed to us. As Jesus noted in his Sermon on the Mount, "You are the light of the world...let your light shine before others, so that they may see your good works and give glory to your Father in heaven" (Matthew 5:14–16).

## The Finding in the Temple

FOCUS: This scene clearly enunciates Jesus' priorities and loyalties, that is, his Father's will. These are the values to which he tenaciously clings, even in the face of bitter opposition and overwhelming disappointment. This seemingly quaint little scene should not be so quaint for us. We too face the issue of ultimate priorities and loyalties. In the face of temptation and catastrophe, we are compelled to make a choice for or against these values. This scene also depicts Mary as perplexed, still wondering about the meaning of her son's words. She confronts unclear revelation—revelation that will only make sense when Jesus is glorified. In the meantime, she must journey in faith and hope, notwithstanding her concerns and worries. We must admit that we also travel the same road.

TEXT: Luke 2:41–52

TEXTUAL EXPLANATION: This passage is a transitional story from the Presentation (Luke 2:22–40) to the beginning of the ministry of Jesus (Luke 3:1). Its purpose is Christological, since it foreshadows the mystery that will culminate in the resurrection and exaltation. Stories of this type are at home in other literatures. There too they allow the reader to glimpse the greatness of the person at an early age. As for this story, Luke has built it around the saying in verse 49 that provokes the failure to understand the revelation in verse 50.

Luke mentions for the first time the going up from Nazareth to Jerusalem. He is probably anticipating the journey in the ministry of Jesus that will bring him to Jerusalem at Passover (Luke 9:51—19:28). The listening and the asking of questions speak to the future when Jesus will openly engage in such debate, although the atmosphere is peaceful here. The astonishment of his parents foreshadows the astonishment of others at the start of Jesus' ministry (Luke 4:32) and the amazement of the scribes at his answer (Luke 20:26). Jesus' reply to his parents indicates that his first allegiance is to his Father's will, not to his family's feelings. "My Father's house" (2:49) identifies Jesus as God's Son.

In verses 51 and 52, Luke softens somewhat the sharpness of verse 49. He presents Jesus as a model of piety who observes the fourth commandment and only exceptionally answers his parents back. He also depicts Mary as open to the mystery of her son. "His mother treasured all these things in her heart" (2:51) provides a place for Mary as a member of Jesus' community (Acts 1:14). Mary symbolizes the early Christian community. She too was searching for a better expression of what she had sensed all along. The scene in the Temple shows that her son's question called for a change in her. Acts 1:14 reveals that she was prepared for that change.

**REFLECTIONS:** This seemingly quaint story is rich in foreshadowing Jesus' sense of priorities. Dedication and commitment to his Father take precedence over family allegiance and loyalty. At the tender age of twelve, Luke reveals Jesus as one who is very much aware of his Father's will. Once that will becomes clear, Jesus never veers from it. For example, in his agony in the garden he prays: "Father, if you are willing, remove this cup from me; yet, not my will but yours be done" (22:42). This resolute Jesus must move us to reassess our own values and priorities. At prayer we are urged to ask this lingering question: Where does my ultimate loyalty lie?

Luke presents Mary as not fully aware of Jesus' mission and destiny. At his birth Luke writes that she "treasured all these words and pondered them in her heart" (2:19). When Simeon proclaims Jesus as a light to the gentiles and glory for Israel (2:33), Mary is utterly amazed. In this present scene where Jesus' loyalty to his Father overwhelms her, Luke once again underlines Mary's predicament; she "treasured all these things in her heart" (2:51). For Luke, Mary confronts unclear revelation she is unable to penetrate. We are reminded of Jacob/Israel in the Greek Old Testament who, after Joseph's dream about the sun, moon, and stars (Genesis 37:9), puzzled over its meaning (Genesis 37:11).

Mary will interpret all these events correctly only after Jesus is enthroned in heaven. For the moment, however, she must hear this word and keep it (see Luke 11:28).

As we reflect in prayer on our own lives, we realize that we are often in a maze or labyrinth in which there appears to be no connection between events. These scenes where Mary ponders and reflects remind us that we must exercise the same patience, faith, and hope as Mary. For the moment, we see indistinctly (1 Corinthians 13:12). Perfect vision still continues to elude us.

# CHAPTER TWO

# THE LUMINOUS MYSTERIES

## The Baptism of Jesus in the Jordan

FOCUS: Rites of passage are common experiences for all of us. We begin a new job, or we get married and start a family. We decide upon a career and determine to remain single. We may become members of a religious community or seek ordination for service in the Church. In all these and similar situations, we are not unlike Jesus at the Jordan. Like him, we have reached a turning point in our lives. Like him, we must interpret our calling. Will our new rite of passage mean serving others, or will it merely be the pursuit of our purely selfish ends? Jesus' baptism is seen as a fresh beginning that is also part of ongoing creation. Do we see ourselves as contributing to this new but ongoing reality? Are we fully aware that every demonstration of genuine human love, in whatever form, continues what God did in the beginning? Will we be partners with this Jesus of the Jordan?

**TEXTS:** Matthew 3:13–17; Mark 1:9–11; Luke 3:21–22

**TEXTUAL EXPLANATION:** To be sure, there are obvious differences among the Synoptic Gospels. For example, in Mark 1:11, the heavenly voice addresses only Jesus. The same is true in Luke 3:22, although the presence of other baptismal candidates makes the scene public. However, in Matthew 3:17 the heavenly voice proclaims Jesus' sonship to the audience in attendance. Matthew and Luke have adapted the text of Mark in other ways. Thus, after Jesus was baptized, he was praying (Luke 3:21). In order to control the embarrassment of the baptism (a baptism of repentance for the remission of sins), Matthew introduces a conversation between Jesus and the Baptist to demonstrate the appropriateness of Jesus' request (3:14–15).

All three accounts, however, preserve early Christian interpretations of Jesus' baptism. Given the fact of the baptism, early Christians sought to interpret who Jesus is. All these accounts, therefore, provide a wealth of Old Testament texts that endeavor to show the various facets of Jesus' person and mission.

The heavenly voice announces that Jesus is truly God's Son. Psalm 2:7, a royal psalm used for the coronation of the Davidic king/Messiah, has God address these words to the new Messiah: "You are my son; today I have begotten you." Jesus, God's Son, is the promised Davidic Messiah. The designation of the Son as "beloved" may allude to Isaac, Abraham's beloved son (Genesis 22:2), and possibly anticipate the sacrifice on the cross. The phrase "with you

I am well pleased" is borrowed from the first Suffering Servant song: "Here is my servant, whom I uphold, my chosen, in whom my soul delights..." (Isaiah 42:1). The prophet envisions this servant as empowered by God's Spirit to effect the reestablishment of the covenant people of Israel. As such, Jesus is commissioned to regather and regroup a scattered Israel.

The setting (the bank of a river), the opening of the heavens, and the heavily symbolic vision of the call to prophetic ministry on behalf of a sinful Israel cannot help but remind us of the prophet Ezekiel by the river Chebar (Ezekial 1:1). Finally, the rending of the heavens that permits God to descend is clearly linked to Isaiah 64:1: O that you would tear open the heavens and come down..." This passage also mentions the role of Moses at the Red Sea and God's gift of the spirit to Israel (Isaiah 63:11, 14). The overall message of this divine announcement is that this Son of God, who is the royal Davidic Messiah, receives an anointing with God's Spirit to exercise a ministry as the final prophet and servant of the Lord on behalf of the sinful people of Israel.

REFLECTIONS: Jesus' baptism undoubtedly serves as a watershed in his life. It marks the point of no return in that Jesus abandons his occupation and family in Nazareth to embrace a ministry clearly at odds with his upbringing. It is hardly a surprise that his townspeople were both amazed and scandalized (Mark 6:1–6). Like Jesus, we too experience radical turning points in our lives such as marriage, remarriage, parenthood, single parenthood, a new job, life as a single person, profession of vows, ordination to service in the Church, and so forth. However, the troubling question is: How shall we interpret these callings? At prayer we must examine whether or not we view ourselves as persons for others. The divine proclamation at the Jordan identifies Jesus as the Spirit-laden prophet and servant of the Lord, whose ministry is directed to the scattered and depleted people of Israel. At prayer, while we acknowledge that we have received the Spirit, we must further probe to what extent that gift of the Spirit has been the catalyst for our service to others. To what extent, therefore, are others the beneficiaries of our prophetic call?

The baptism at the Jordan brings together the following elements: water, spirit, and bird (dove). If we consult Genesis 1:2, the first creation account, we have a mighty wind/spirit hovering over the waters. The hovering implies the image of a bird, for example, in Deuteronomy 32:11: "As an eagle stirs up its nest, and hovers over its young…" For early Christians, the baptism of Jesus conjured the end time as a new beginning. They understood Jesus at his baptism to be the bringer of a new creation. As in the first creation, God's Spirit now hovers over the Jordan. The outcome is the new age that is set in motion.

The Bible sees creation as an ongoing reality. What God did in the beginning was simply that—a beginning. For example, the prophet Second Isaiah preached a message of hope to his beleaguered exiles in Babylon by assuring them that they would return home. This act of redemption is subsumed under the category of creation. "But now thus says the Lord, he who created you, O Jacob, he who formed you, O Israel: Do not fear, for I have redeemed you; I have called you by name, you are mine" (Isaiah 43:1). In view of this doctrine, we can declare that creation continues whenever there is genuine human love. Whenever we overcome the chaos that can rule our lives, whenever we offer hope and consolation to the depressed and despairing, we make creation ongoing. We too are called upon to breathe the Spirit that makes genuine human living a reality. To that extent we too are plunged into the Jordan and receive the daily commission to regroup the scattered people in our lives. In this way creation is still alive and well.

## The Wedding Feast at Cana

FOCUS: It is all too easy to get hung up on the idea of one hundred twenty gallons of wine. The author of John encourages us to see in this abundance of wine something more than an embarrassment-saving feat. By looking more deeply into this episode, we catch a glimpse of Jesus' glory that will be only fully revealed on Calvary. The plentiful wine points to the final messianic times and hence Jesus' messiahship. We are also urged to reflect on this abundance as Jesus' wisdom and teaching.

Is Jesus my personal savior and nothing more? In other words, do I view my faith as a legacy that belongs only to me and no one else? This passage demands that we appreciate the author's depiction of Mary's faith. The account reveals her faith in Jesus, but does not stop there. It is also a profound faith that enables the disciples to come to faith in Jesus. We are, therefore, bidden to understand this "woman" against the background of community. As the mother of Jesus, she is bound up with all the concerns and needs of his sisters and brothers.

**TEXT:** John 2:1–12

**TEXTUAL EXPLANATION:** The story of the wedding feast at Cana is part of the Book of Signs (John 1:19—12:50). In the Fourth Gospel sign is the Johannine term for a miracle. However, the accent here lies not in the amazing feats accomplished by Jesus, but in the manifestation of divine glory. Hence one must look beyond the event to discover its significance and value. Although it is very difficult to reconstruct this scene historically, what does emerge is the revelation of the person of Jesus and the faith of Jesus' mother and the disciples.

The wine—some one hundred twenty gallons—has a Christological purpose that John elaborates by the use of symbols. Jesus brings to fulfillment Jewish feasts and ceremonies—here the prescriptions of Jewish purification— with an abundance of wine. Since Jesus is the only way to the Father, Jewish customs and practices attain their fullest meaning in him. The wedding feast symbolizes messianic days. In Isaiah 62:4–5, the prophet speaks of the coming marriage between the Lord and Jerusalem. Amos 9:13–14 refers to the abundance of wine that will characterize "the coming days." John may also be alluding to Jesus' role as

Wisdom in Providence 9:5, where Lady Wisdom beckons to her followers to drink of her wine.

Mary plays a crucial role in this scene. In saying to the servers, "Do whatever he tells you," (2:5), Mary (identified only as the "mother of Jesus" and "woman") is the very first to come to faith. With this command, she clearly exhibits and communicates her faith to others. She is the catalyst by which Jesus reveals his glory and the disciples start to believe in him. She also initiates the "hour" of Jesus, that is, the moment that comprises the passion and death of Jesus, but also his glorification in his resurrection and return to the Father. Mary will appear only once more in this gospel when the "hour" demands her presence on Calvary with the beloved disciple (John 19:25–27). There she will assist in the birth of a new people of God. Mary, the woman of faith, is the key link between the beginning and end of this gospel.

REFLECTIONS: This passage is the unmistakable invitation to view Jesus as the total revelation of the Father and thereby to accept his message. In this sense, we may rightly speak of Jesus as the great communicator. As the conclusion of the prologue puts it, "No one has ever seen God. It is God the only Son, who is close to the Father's heart, who has made him known" (John 1:18). The impact from this revelation and its acceptance cannot be expressed in so many words. It can only be grasped in symbols. The approximately one hundred twenty gallons of wine attempt to capture symbolically the dynamism and awesomeness of committing oneself in faith to this great communicator.

We are also reminded of the role of Mary and her contribution to the message of Jesus. According to John she is the very first person to come to faith by uttering, "Do whatever he tells you" (2:5). However, her faith is not a purely private possession but a communal patrimony. She perceives the needs of others and addresses them. She shares this attitude of faith with the disciples of Jesus so that Jesus can reveal himself, and they can begin to believe. This woman at Cana challenges us to share our faith with others. What we have received is ultimately for the good of others. Like Mary, we are asked to be catalysts whereby the awesome revelation of Jesus reaches ever new audiences. The woman at Cana can only be adequately understood in terms of Jesus' extended family. We are the commissioned sisters and brothers of that family.

## The Proclamation of the Kingdom

**FOCUS:** Besides faith, we are also in dire need of hope. As in the parable of the seed, we perfectly understand how things go wrong, but not how they go right. In spite of failures, we must dare to hope in bumper crops. Basically hope means the acceptance of and commitment to a God of surprises. This is a God who challenges us to look beyond past disappointments. Our God is not constrained to operate according to our iron laws of energy expended and results obtained.

What kind of a future does the kingdom hold for believers? The parable of the buried treasure urges us to envision a world of new possibilities grounded in the person of Jesus the parabler. By accepting the values of Jesus, the parable of God, we can indeed turn our lives around. Reversals can become the order of the day because of the great discovery.

TEXT: Matthew 13:1–9, 44–46

TEXTUAL EXPLANATION: The expression "kingdom of God" (Matthew usually prefers "kingdom of heaven") emphasizes the notion that God is sovereign over all humanity and creation. It is connected to the "Day of the Lord," the hope of a demonstration of God's kingly rule that brings peace, harmony, and abundance (Isaiah 2:2–4; Micah 4:1–4). It is interesting that Jesus hardly ever explains the meaning of kingship or kingdom. However, his own parables show the kingdom as a reality of God's involvement with human beings. Several of the parables in Matthew provide good examples of such involvement.

Verses 3–9, the parable of the seed, not the sower, deal with the natural inevitability of failure and success in sowing. There are three states of loss: immediate (path), gradual (rocks), and ultimate (thorns). There are three degrees of gain in the good soil: thirty, sixty, and one hundred (hence as diverse as the losses). Significantly, the parable spells out how things go wrong (path, rocks, thorns) but not how they go right. The parable points to the law of growth and decline in the kingdom. Although one can understand better how things go wrong, one is challenged to hope in that mysterious process whereby they go right. God's plan is at work: good results do come, although the bad ones are more readily explained.

The parables of the buried treasure and the pearl (13:44–46) are unique to Matthew. Both deal with the advent of the kingdom and radical commitment to it, for example, the selling of everything one has. Both have the same sequence: finding, selling, buying. Yet at the same time, they are different. In the first parable, the farmer is not seeking but happens to find the treasure. In the second parable, the merchant is seeking and finally finds his pearl. In the first there is a certain shock in that the farmer hides the treasure and goes off to buy a seemingly ordinary field. In the second there is less shock, since the merchant goes about his purchase quite openly.

In the treasure parable, the first stage is normalcy, the routine work of a farmer whose whole future is determined by his circumstances. The second stage is the discovery of the treasure that then creates a new world and new possibilities. The third stage is the reversal of the past, whereby the farmer is obliged to sell everything he has. The fourth stage is the new activity of the farmer made possible by the discovery. He is no longer programmed as before. This fourth stage is the world that Jesus offers his disciples. The kingdom is a world of new possibilities grounded in the person of Jesus.

REFLECTIONS: The parable of the seed confirms our typically human experience—we can explain better how things go wrong than how things go right. However, hope is a central virtue for all those who heed Jesus, the preacher of God's kingdom. Hope enables us to restore God's capacity to surprise us. Despite failures and disappointments, our God is one who makes possible bumper crops of thirty-fold, sixty-fold, and even a hundredfold. In the kingdom, our iron laws of success and failure are not applicable, since our God operates in truly mysterious ways. To be surprised is to acknowledge that our God cannot be constrained by our standard operating procedures.

The parable of the buried treasure reminds us that the world that Jesus offers his followers is a world of new possibilities that is grounded in his person. In this parable, Jesus extends an invitation to embrace a new future that is linked to his kingdom message. We are challenged to reorient our lives as a result of the discovery of that message. The values and principles of this kingdom preacher are to become our values and principles by daily effort. We are not to hide that treasure, but to make it available to our community. Such a treasure must become contagious.

## The Transfiguration

FOCUS: Pain, tragedy, and misfortune: Are they merely to be endured with a stiff upper lip? Are they totally divorced from our journey in faith? Jesus' transfiguration challenges us to see all these upsetting events as the raw material for fulfillment. By coping as Jesus did, we are able to complete our mission by embracing these moments as transforming experiences. We can perhaps begin to see them as essential components of our journey. Death will not have the final word.

What about our sisters and brothers who seem almost to despair in the face of enormous crises? Our task is certainly not to attempt to explain or clarify the reality of such experiences. Jesus' transfiguration suggests, rather, that we offer consolation and hope. As a family of believers, we must create ways in which our sisters and brothers make the transition from despair to hope.

TEXTS: Matthew 17:1–8; Mark 9:2–8; Luke 9:28–36

TEXTUAL EXPLANATION: On a literary level, the Synoptic accounts of the transfiguration may be classified as an epiphany. In such a literary form, there is a sudden and unexpected appearance of a divine or heavenly being in which that being communicates a divine attribute, action, or message. In this epiphany, the focus is on a specific command, "listen to him." The event is also pivotal since the command occurs at a key point in the gospel narrative, after the first prediction of the passion of Jesus. Jesus' change into a heavenly figure provides an easy transition to his appearance and conversation with Moses and Elijah, who are already members of this heavenly realm. For example, in Gabriel's appearance to Daniel, the angel's face shines like lightning (Daniel 10:6), while Jesus' face shines like the sun (Matthew 17:2). In another of Daniel's visions, the clothing of the Ancient One (God) is snow bright (Daniel 7:9), while Jesus' clothing becomes white as light (Matthew 17:2).

What is significant is the way in which Moses and Elijah attained heavenly glory. According to 2 Kings 2:11, Elijah went up to heaven in a whirlwind. According to Deuteronomy 34:7, Moses was one hundred twenty years old at the time of his death on Mount Nebo, and "his sight was unimpaired and his vigor had not abated." In first-century AD Jewish tradition, Moses never really died, but merely disappeared and returned to God. According to another tradition in this same time period, Moses did not suffer the hideous death of a rejected prophet. Rather, he died in glory and entered heaven at such time. What is noteworthy here is that Jesus, unlike Moses and Elijah, will achieve heavenly glory not by avoiding death or dying a natural death, but by undergoing death at the hands of his own people as a completely innocent and righteous prophet.

On an historical level, it is difficult to determine what actually happened in this episode. One proposal is the following: Aware that his enemies were gaining the upper hand and would probably bring about his death, Jesus withdrew to the top of a mountain to pray. At this moment of very intense prayer, Jesus received his answer and his face lit up. Although he previously thought that he would not complete his mission by dying, he now realized that his death would be the means of fulfilling that ministry. Like the suffering servant in Isaiah 52:13—53:12, he saw that his death would benefit humanity. He also realized that he would be exonerated: "See, my servant shall prosper; he shall be exalted and lifted up" (Isaiah 52:13). Like the righteous sufferer in the Book of Wisdom, Jesus now understood that his Father would intervene on his behalf: "For if the righteous man is God's child, he will help him, and will deliver him from the hand of his adversaries" (Wisdom 2:18).

REFLECTIONS: This scene on the top of the mountain provides new insight and meaning to suffering and death. For us, as for Jesus, heavenly glory is not simply a mere reward that is totally devoid of any connection with our real life experiences. Heaven is not simply the place for our souls—it is also the place for our bodies. Heavenly glory is not based on our desire to avoid, but in our courage and boldness, to accept rejection, pain, and finally death. Heaven hinges on all our human experiences, especially the most demanding ones. The author of Hebrew who places Jesus on a level with the God of Israel (Hebrews 1:8) underlines his utter humanity as he grapples with hurt and pain. "Because he himself was tested by what he suffered, he is able to help those who are being tested" (Hebrews 2:18). In his transfiguration, Jesus is our model for coping with the shocks, disappointments, and frustrations of human experience.

Since we are always joined to our sisters and brothers, the transfiguration offers a challenge not only to cope with our own sufferings, but also with those of Jesus' extended family. In this episode, Jesus saw that there was light at the end of the tunnel, that his violent death would not be God's final act. Too many of our sisters and brothers, implicitly at least, reach out to us to help them make the transition from pain to glory. Our encouragement, our physical and financial assistance, our message of hope, and so forth are the means by which light begins to break through and our distraught family members start to see that their pain can be the springboard to life on a new level. Our mission, therefore, is to make faces light up. By the time our sisters and brothers reach the bottom of the mountain, life is no longer just a drudgery but a series of faith-filled moments.

## The Eucharist

FOCUS: When we celebrate the Eucharist, which aspect do we usually emphasize—the communal or the personal? In First Corinthians, Paul invites us to stress the communal dimension. In proclaiming the death of the Lord, we assume the posture of Jesus' self-giving. When we truly remember Jesus, we include all humanity, not merely ourselves.

On the other hand, the Gospel of John underlines the personal aspect of the Eucharist. We are intimately connected with Jesus in the mission committed to him by his Father. Jesus, as the bread of life, becomes the basis of eternal life for us now. We thus personally participate in the life of the Trinity.

TEXTS: Matthew 26:26–29; Mark 14:22–25; Luke 22:15–20; John 6:30–59; 1 Corinthians 11:17–34

TEXTUAL EXPLANATION: First Corinthians is our earliest biblical record of the Eucharist. (Luke's Eucharist tradition is close to Paul's with some exceptions.) Interestingly, it was a situation of Eucharist abuse that provided the occasion for Paul's understanding of this central Christian ritual. In Corinth, the Eucharist followed a regular meal. However, the Christian social elite arrived first and received the utmost in hospitality from the host, including a private room where they could recline for their meal. Only later were the lower Christian classes able to show up for the regular meal. However, they sat in the courtyard and were treated to only second-class fare. Not surprisingly, Paul observes that "one goes hungry and another becomes drunk" (11:21).

In the words of institution, Paul twice uses the phrase "in remembrance of me" (11:24–25). This is not a perfunctory recollection of the events of Good Friday. Rather, it is the recalling of the deeper meaning of Jesus' dying. Jesus' self-giving plunges the believer into a sharing of life, not only with the Lord, but also with the other participants. Paul heightens this sense of remembrance when he notes that in Eucharist one proclaims the death of the Lord (11:26). For Paul the death of Jesus is the unambiguous expression of Jesus' love for humanity (see Galatians 2:20). That dying, the ultimate demonstration of concern for and involvement with others, becomes the model for ongoing Christian living. As Paul says elsewhere, we no longer live for ourselves but for Christ (shorthand for the Christian community), who died and was raised for us (2 Corinthians 5:15). The class distinctions at Corinth that disparaged the lower classes and catered to the elite contradicted the central reality of Eucharist.

At the Last Supper, Mark uses the categories of covenant and sacrifice. (With some exceptions, Matthew follows Mark rather closely.) When Jesus gives the broken pieces of bread to the disciples, he intends the action to symbolize their sharing in his self-offering. "My blood of the covenant" (14:24) alludes to Exodus 24:3–8. The disciples enter into a covenant relationship with Jesus by drinking the cup. By means of this symbolic action, Jesus is seen as interpreting his mission in terms of self-offering for the Semitic "many," that is, all. This expression, together with the "pouring out" (14:24), is a link to The Suffering Servant (Isaiah 52:13—53:12). The Eucharist is thus understood as a new source of life by which one shares community with Jesus. At the same time, there is the tension of anticipation. The disciples are to look forward to that final banquet over which Jesus presides in God's kingdom.

In the Gospel of John, there is no institution of the Eucharist at the Last Supper. Instead, John employs the multiplication of the loaves and fish in 6:1–15 to introduce his bread of life discourse. In verses 31–35, Jesus points out that the real bread from heaven is not the manna that the ancestors of his Jewish audience ate. Rather, the real bread from heaven is Jesus himself. "I am the bread of life. Whoever comes to me will never be hungry, and whoever believes in me will never be thirsty" (6:35). Jesus, as the bread of life, is the very embodiment of God's revelation.

In verses 51–58. Jesus passes from the use of bread for symbolizing his identity to its sacramental use. It is now a question of eating the flesh and drinking the blood of Jesus. In the Old Testament, "flesh and blood" expresses human life. The separate mention of the flesh and the blood probably suggests that in the Eucharist, the believer receives the whole living Jesus. Here John emphasizes the personal more than the communal dimension of Eucharist. By sharing in the Eucharist, the believer shares in the life of Father, Son, and Spirit (see John 15:26). The result of this sharing is the establishment of an eternal relationship with God. Eucharist is for living now, so that one can continue to live. By contrast, the manna in the desert is only a very weak analogy.

**REFLECTIONS:** In Paul's theology, Eucharist is a risk-filled undertaking, since it involves us not only with Jesus but with the entire community. In Eucharist we are challenged to proclaim the death of the Lord by reaching out to all the members of the Eucharistic celebration. We truly remember Jesus when we remember his sisters and brothers, especially the non-elite who suffer from disregard and neglect. To eat and drink with Jesus is to become food and drink for his extended family. In this sense, Eucharist removes us from the realm of sacred liturgy to the arena of sacred activity. In the troublesome and vexing moments of daily life, we find the raw material for nourishing and sustaining our sisters and brothers. The Pauline Eucharist, though filled with risks and dangers, is the faith opportunity to proclaim in action what we profess in words.

In John's theology, Eucharist has a more personal dimension in that the individual believer shares more intimately with Jesus in the saving mission committed to him by his Father. "Just as the living Father sent me, and I live because of the Father, so whoever eats me will live because of me" (6:57). Jesus, as the bread of life, becomes the foundation of eternal life now and the promise of the resurrection at his Second Coming. Elsewhere (John 14:10–11; 17:21, 23) John teaches that the relationship between Jesus and his disciples reflects that between Jesus and his Father. In turn, Eucharist becomes the sign of that relationship and further undergirds it.

# CHAPTER THREE

# THE SORROWFUL MYSTERIES

## The Agony in the Garden

FOCUS: The clash of wills is at the center of Jesus' prayer in the Synoptic gospels. We know our own preferences and are naturally inclined to follow them. The cup of pain and suffering can be so overwhelming that we would opt not to think of it at all. At this point we have to reach deep within ourselves and seek to have God's will prevail. This is the stance of the disciple, not on a few unique occasions, but in daily life situations.

Mary, the Mother of Jesus, is not mentioned in any of the garden scenes. However, we know from Luke that a sword will pierce her as Jesus is rejected by his people. Elsewhere we encounter her grappling with unclear revelation at Jesus' birth and his finding in the Temple. She too has to find her inner strength in total openness to God's plan and her capacity to hope despite dismal circumstances.

TEXTS: Matthew 26:36–46; Mark 14:32–42; Luke 22:39–46; John 18:1–11

TEXTUAL EXPLANATION: Mark paints a stark picture of gloom and tragedy as Jesus approaches Gethsemane. He has already foretold Peter's denial (14:27–31) and betrayal by one of the Twelve (14:17–21). Separating Peter, James, and John from the rest of the disciples, Jesus informs them that he is deeply grieved to the point of death. Jesus' posture captures his desperate state—he falls to the ground. He is indeed troubled and distressed. From the depths of his humanity, he addresses his Father in prayer, asking that this cup/hour may pass by him. However, he emphatically insists on the priority of his Father's will. Hoping to find support from his disciples, he discovers to his chagrin that they are sound asleep. Although he had earlier urged watchfulness and vigilance (13:32–37), he must repeat that message at this critical moment. Apparently it is to no avail as their slumber continues. After further prayer, he rises fully determined to accept the will of his Father.

Like Mark, Matthew separates the three special disciples from the rest and portrays Jesus' experience of sorrow and distress. However, Matthew changes Jesus' posture—he falls on his face to the earth. Such a position is used in the Old Testament to reflect adoration and respect (see Genesis 17:3; 2 Samuel 9:6). His prayer to the Father ("My Father,…yet not what I want but what you want" [26:39]) echoes the Our Father (Matthew 6:9–10). Throughout the gospel, therefore, Jesus' relationship with his Father remains steadfast. What is particularly noteworthy in Matthew's account is the emphasis on Jesus' association with the disciples. Whereas Mark has Jesus find "them" and speak "to them" (Mark 14:37, 41) after the first and third prayer, Matthew employs nouns instead of pronouns, for example, "to the disciples" (26:40, 45). Whereas the Markan Jesus instructs the three disciples to keep watch and questions Peter about keeping watch (Mark 14:34, 37), the Matthean Jesus commands the three to "stay awake with me" (26:38, 40). It is clear that Matthew has elected to emphasize the bond between Jesus and his disciples, although, at this time of trial, they too fail to respond. As in Mark, Jesus advances from sorrow and distress to the firm resolve to embrace his Father's will. One gets the impression that his determination increases with each moment of prayer.

In Luke, the Mount of Olives is a customary place for Jesus. Unlike the Markan and Matthean Jesus, the Lukan Jesus does not remove himself from the disciples as a whole and then from the special threesome. In addition, the Lukan Jesus finds the disciples asleep only once, not three times. Once again, Jesus' posture is significant. He does not fall on the ground as in Mark. Rather, he kneels—a posture that suggests that he is in greater control of himself. Unlike Mark, Luke has Jesus pray only once, not three times. Thus Jesus apparently realizes rather quickly the will of his Father. More importantly, Luke omits Mark's description of Jesus as deeply grieved. For Luke's audience, such a state has negative connotations of sin and punishment. (Such a negative judgment is appropriate for the disciples in verse

45 who are sleeping because of grief.) Luke goes on to mention the assistance of a strengthening angel. Whereas both Mark 1:13 and Matthew 4:11 narrate the service of angels at the conclusion of the temptation in the desert, Luke has reserved such assistance for the time of the passion. The term "agony" implies contest, struggle, gymnastic exercise. Hence Jesus is involved in a type of combat and ordeal. Since the angel strengthens Jesus in this struggle, he is not under the influence of grief that typically diminishes such strength. At the end of this scene, Jesus emerges stronger and ever more resolved to accept the cup.

In the Gospel of John, there is no ordeal or agony in the garden. There is no need for prayer at this moment, since the Father and Jesus are one (John 10:30). Instead, John has Jesus reject the petition to his Father to save him during the time of the ministry. "And what should I say? 'Father, save me from this hour'? No, it was for this reason that I have come to this hour" (John 12:27). The Johannine Jesus is in complete control of himself and the situation during the passion. Indeed he is anxious to drink the cup that the Father has prepared for him (John 18:11).

REFLECTIONS: With which Jesus can we identify when we have a conflict between our own will and God's will at prayer? Perhaps it is the Markan Jesus more often than not. Distraught we fall to the ground, trying to discover a route or destiny other than God's. We thus plead: "...remove this cup from me..." (Mark 14:36). Perhaps all too reluctantly we finally choose God's will over our own. It is possible that the Matthean Jesus better suits us. Instead of falling to the ground, we fall on our face to the earth, adopting a posture that suggests respect. Instead of demanding outright our own will, we may begin more cautiously with a condition, that is, if it is possible. But we then qualify it with: "...yet not what I want but what you want" (Matthew 26:39). If we are more resolute in preferring God's will to our own, we can then identify with the Lukan Jesus. Our posture of kneeling may imply our openness to God's plan and thus the need to utter only one prayer, not three prayers. We acknowledge that we are in a combat mode but are reassured and strengthened by God's presence in the form of an angel. God's will, not our own, has prevailed. No doubt the most difficult Jesus to identify with is the Johannine Jesus. Since the Father and he are one, their wills are one. Prayer is really not necessary, since from the very start God's will has won out over our own. The outcome is set. Victory will eventually come since God's will has prevailed.

As we try to fathom God's will for whatever situation, we may find comfort in reflecting on the Lukan Mary, the mother of Jesus. At Jesus' birth and at his discovery at age twelve in the Temple, she is found to be keeping all these things in her heart. She is the recipient of unclear revelation, unaware of the deeper meaning of these events. Though she is puzzled, she remains the woman of faith, exhibiting patience to the "nth" degree. Only in the light of Jesus' exaltation will she grasp the full meaning. This model disciple of Luke surely has much to teach us.

# The Scourging

**FOCUS:** Scourging as a preliminary to crucifixion raises the specter of Roman capital punishment. Reserved generally for low life, this form of death was degrading and appalling—according to Paul, a stumbling block for Jews and utter foolishness for gentiles. As we ponder the scourging within the context of crucifixion, we must dare to ask what is positive about this form of torture. Does God once again exhibit the ability to take what is horrendous and despicable and change it into an expression of the deepest love? Does this element of the passion signal divine compassion for humanity?

**TEXTS:** Matthew 27:26; Mark 15:15; Luke 23:16, 22; John 19:1

**TEXTUAL EXPLANATION:** Crucifixion was a Roman form of capital punishment that subjected the victim to the maximum indignity. The Church father Origen spoke of crucifixion as the utterly vile death of the cross. Used as a deterrent because of its harshness, it was almost always inflicted on the lower classes. Such classes would include slaves, violent criminals, and unruly elements in the provinces. It was also a type of punishment in which the sadism of the executioners knew no bounds or restraints. For Greeks, Romans, barbarians, and Jews the cross symbolized a totally offensive action against a human being. Given this attitude, a crucified Messiah was a contradiction in terms.

Against such a background Paul did not hesitate to preach: "but we proclaim Christ crucified, a stumbling block to Jews and foolishness to gentiles" (1 Corinthians 1:23). According to the interpretation of Deuteronomy 21:23 in the first century AD, God's curse on one who hangs on a tree included anyone crucified. Paul, however, detects a certain irony in Jesus' death by crucifixion since, by becoming a curse for humanity, Jesus brought freedom from the curse of the Jewish law (Galatians 3:13). In Philippians, Paul cites a hymn that emphasizes Jesus' obedience unto death, but he qualifies that death by inserting the phrase "even death on a cross" (Philippians 2:8). In Romans 8:32, Paul also remarks that in the death of Jesus, God identified himself with the very extreme of human misery. Paradoxically, the crucified Christ is the very power and wisdom of God (1 Corinthians 1:24).

Unlike the apocryphal gospels and some canonical writings, for example, 2 Maccabees 7:1–42, these gospel accounts do not focus on the extreme pain and suffering that Jesus experienced. Their interest lies elsewhere, in the Old Testament psalms and prophets. They choose, therefore, not to provide gory biographical details, but to interpret the significance of Jesus' passion and death. Through the Jewish Scriptures, God says so much about his Son.

Scourging a prisoner prior to his or her death on the cross was a widespread Roman custom. As a matter of fact, it was part of the very sentence of crucifixion. The scourges used by the executioners were frequently fitted with pieces of bone or metal, with the result that the condemned could suffer enormous pain. According to the Jewish historian Josephus, some condemned actually died as a result of the scourging. Among the evangelists only Matthew and Mark mention that Jesus was scourged at the end of his Roman trial as a preliminary to his execution. According to Luke 23:16, Pilate intends to have Jesus scourged as a form of chastisement since he finds him not guilty of any capital offense. Although Pilate repeats his intention in Luke 23:22, the Lukan Jesus is never scourged. According to John 19:1, Pilate has Jesus scourged. However, this is not a preliminary to crucifixion, but a ploy by Pilate to move the crowd to accept Jesus' release.

**REFLECTIONS:** While the cross was the instrument of degradation for non-believers, it became for Christians the great symbol of love. While opponents claimed that Christians worshipped a criminal who died on the tree of shame, Christians themselves responded that the cross captured the greatest expression of God's involvement with humanity. Paul announces confidently that, despite all the obstacles and threats to salvation and union with God, the cross assures us of ultimate victory. "He who did not withhold his own Son, but gave him up for all of us, will he not with him also give us everything else?" (Romans 8:32). In the final analysis the cross is neither a stumbling block nor foolishness. Rather, it is the most concrete proof of God's overwhelming love.

# The Crowning with Thorns

FOCUS: How do we recognize this Jesus who is the object of such humiliation and mockery? We do not have to look far to discover this Jesus. He is disguised in all hurting and downtrodden sisters and brothers. Unfortunately the ridicule of Jesus persists wherever people suffer the loss of their basic human dignity. To reflect on this aspect of the passion is to situate ourselves in any circumstance where injustice prevails. This mocked Jesus is sadly all too alive and well in our midst.

TEXTS: Matthew 27:27–31; Mark 15:16–20; Luke 23:11; John 19:2–3

TEXTUAL EXPLANATION: In both Matthew and Mark, the crowning with thorns is part of the mockery by the Roman soldiers. Although Pilate did not order such mockery, the soldiers appear to engage in it spontaneously. In Mark, Jesus is clothed in royal purple, while in Matthew, he wears a scarlet military cloak. With regard to the crown of thorns (it is more of a wreath or diadem than a crown), there is no intent to torture. It is simply another component in the royal mockery. In Mark, the reed functions as an instrument for striking Jesus' head. In Matthew, however, the reed initially serves as a mock scepter. Only afterwards is it employed to hit Jesus. In both Matthew and Mark, Jesus is accorded the salutation "Hail, King of the Jews," a taunt that reminds the reader of "Hail, Caesar." Matthew mentions kneeling as an element in reviling Jesus—something that Mark records only after the abuse. In both Matthew and Mark, spitting is another element in this humiliating scene, and both note that Jesus is dressed again in his own clothes before setting out for the place of execution.

Luke does not have any mockery by the Roman soldiers during or immediately after the Roman trial. However, he does narrate a scene that is wanting in the other three evangelists. Learning that Jesus comes from Galilee, Pilate dispatches him to Herod Antipas, the tetrarch of that area. Refusing to accommodate Herod by performing some sign, Jesus receives only ridicule from the tetrarch and his soldiers. As in Matthew and Mark, clothing figures as an ingredient of the scene. In this case, the garb is resplendent or shining—probably an indication of innocence, not mockery.

John is close to Mark (purple robe) and Matthew (placing the crown on Jesus' head). Unlike Matthew and Mark, John places the mockery in the middle of the Roman trial, not after its conclusion. Like the scourging, the mockery is designed by Pilate to elicit sympathy for the disfigured Jesus. To this end, the Roman soldiers strike him repeatedly. Like Matthew and Mark, John has Jesus greeted derisively as "Hail, King of the Jews."

**REFLECTIONS:** The tragic figure depicted by all four evangelists naturally evokes our sense of both sympathy and outrage. Given the nobility and generosity of Jesus in all four gospel accounts, we are legitimately appalled by the mockery he is forced to endure. We feel that, unlike the crowds in Luke and John, we would accept Pilate's ploy and demand Jesus' release.

But do we dare to see in this disfigured and abused Jesus the image and likeness of our sisters and brothers? According to Luke, the author of the Acts of the Apostles, Jesus addresses Saul on the road to Damascus with this question: "Saul, Saul, why do you persecute me?" (Acts 9:4; 22:7; 26:15). Saul learns that to persecute the Christian community is to persecute Jesus. In First Corinthians, Paul announces to this beleaguered Christian church that the Christian community is the body of Christ. "If one member suffers, all suffer together with it" (12:26). In the Gospel of Matthew, Jesus identifies with the hungry, the thirsty, the naked, the prisoners (25:31–46). Whatever is done for the least sisters and brothers of Jesus is done for Jesus.

Perhaps this message of Luke, Paul, and Matthew is a key for reflecting on the mockery of Jesus. Basically we are challenged to accept a God of disguises, a God who chooses to appear in our distraught sisters and brothers. Pity and sympathy are certainly reasonable reactions to their plight. To be sure, prayer on their behalf is a most worthy response. However, concrete action to relieve their stress must become a necessary component of our reactions. To assist one depressed and hurting human being is to understand this element of the passion narrative. It is also to make the move from Good Friday afternoon to Easter Sunday morning.

## The Carrying of the Cross

FOCUS: What a contrast between the Johannine Jesus and the Lukan Jesus! The Johannine Jesus advances confidently to his death in no need of human assistance. On the other hand, the Lukan Jesus is so weakened that he requires Simon's help if he is going to make it to the execution site. In addition, the Lukan Jesus has the dubious company of two criminals.

How do the women strike us in Luke? The daughters of Jerusalem exhibit a basic human quality that is unfortunately all too scarce in our society: compassion. The sight of this helpless Jesus moves them to tears and wailing. The women sense the unseemliness—rather, the injustice of this entire episode. We must ask if we permit ourselves to be moved by the hopelessness and injustice in our own society. If so, what course of action will we then take?

TEXTS: Matthew 27:31–32; Mark 15:20–21; Luke 23:26–32; John 19:16–17

TEXTUAL EXPLANATION: After the preliminary scourging, the condemned would carry the crossbeam or lateral beam behind his neck with his arms fastened to it to the place of crucifixion and be scourged as he went along. Usually the vertical part of the cross remained fixed in the ground at the execution site. According to Matthew, Mark, and Luke, Simon of Cyrene (presumably an unknown figure) is forced to carry Jesus' crossbeam. This suggests Jesus' severely weakened state as the result of the scourging and other abuse. It is interesting to note that in John there is no need of a Simon of Cyrene, since Jesus carries his own cross. For John this fact is calculated to stress Jesus' total control or authority in the crucifixion. Earlier in this gospel, Jesus had stated: "…I lay down my life in order to take it up again. No one takes it from me, but I lay it down of my own accord" (John 10:17–18).

Luke emphasizes the fact that Simon carried Jesus' cross *behind* or *after* him (23:26). This is the same preposition that Luke used earlier in his instruction on discipleship. For instance, in 9:23 Jesus teaches: "If any want to become my followers (literally: to come behind/after me), let them deny themselves and take up their cross daily and follow me." Simon's service to Jesus in this episode thus becomes an example of genuine discipleship. Jesus' journey to Jerusalem (Luke 9:51—19:28), therefore, culminates in a disciple's gesture on the road to Calvary.

Luke, alone among the evangelists, notes the presence of Jews who are not disciples of Jesus, but who are nonetheless touched by his pitiful condition (23:27). In particular, the women exhibit compassion for Jesus in their mourning and lamenting him. Thus not all of the people reject Jesus. Nevertheless, in addressing these women of Jerusalem, Jesus puts aside his own fate to focus on the catastrophe that awaits this city. This is a city that killed the prophets and refused Jesus' message (Luke 13:34–35). As a result, it will be abandoned and trodden underfoot by its enemies (Luke 19:41–44; 21:20–24).

In calling the barren blessed (see Isaiah 54:1) and citing

the mountains and hills as agents of destruction (see Hosea 10:8), the Lukan Jesus is referring to the tragic destruction of the great city by the Romans in 70 AD. The proverb in verse 31 about the green wood and the dry wood may mean the following: If Jesus, who is innocent, suffers death at the hands of the Romans, what can the guilty expect? Only Luke mentions that two criminals accompanied Jesus on this death march. This may be Luke's way of dramatizing Jesus as the companion of sinners and outcasts.

**REFLECTIONS:** Which Jesus has the greater appeal for us: the Johannine Jesus who carries the cross all by himself or the Lukan Jesus who is assisted by Simon and accompanied by two criminals? To be sure, the Johannine Jesus demonstrates those qualities of strength that we most admire, such as control, nobility, and authority. However, while we can greatly admire this Jesus, can we also imitate him? On the other hand, the Lukan Jesus is attractive in that he exhibits our typically human traits of weakness. He is in desperate need of help and, as a result, has to depend on the assistance of a fellow human. The company of the Lukan Jesus may also remind us of our families and friends. They are people who make mistakes and thus exemplify our human condition. However, for one of the two criminals, association with Jesus will provide the opportunity to enter Jesus' kingdom. In the end we are left with two decidedly different portraits of Jesus. Depending on our situation in life, one may have a greater appeal for us. Though they are in tension, both remain models for the contemporary disciple.

Compassion is at times a difficult virtue to emulate. We prefer to be in complete control of our emotions and not display any kind of involvement. Such a stoic approach tends to keep us well insulated and isolated within our ego. However, the women of Jerusalem do not share this outlook. Distraught by the appearance of the weakened Jesus, they break out in sobs and tears. Such suffering has struck a very sensitive chord in their entire make-up. They are constrained to react. This scene may be a healthy antidote for our own lack of compassion at times. We must ask ourselves whether we should be moved to tears and then to action when we witness the pain and plight of so many people vividly displayed on our television sets. Do we dare to hear the community's desperate cry for help? The Jerusalem women must continue to influence our daily lives.

## The Crucifixion and Death

FOCUS: How should we view Good Friday? Is it simply a tragic event because an innocent man has been put to death? If we look at the Gospel of John, we realize that such an attitude is completely unfounded. When Jesus dies in John, he hands over the Spirit. Good Friday is now Pentecost. While the blood flowing from the side of Jesus dramatizes his death, the water symbolizes the gift of the Spirit.

While Luke does not envision Good Friday as Pentecost, he sees it as much more than a senseless tragedy. On the cross, Jesus speaks words of forgiveness that are directed to those responsible for his death. Moreover, he throws open the gates of paradise to the repentant criminal. Against a background of Good Friday gloom, there is also the manifestation of grace.

**TEXTS:** Matthew 27:33–56; Mark 15:22–41; Luke 23:33–49; John 19:17–37

**TEXTUAL EXPLANATION:** One may describe Mark's account of the crucifixion and death of Jesus as an expose of the shocking facts that occurred on Good Friday. At the same time, however, it is an account full of paradox and mystery, one designed to evoke from the reader the centurion's profession of faith: "Truly this man was God's Son!" (15:39).

While Matthew follows Mark closely, he departs from his source when discussing the repercussions following Jesus' death in 27:51–53. Besides the tearing of the Temple curtain, Matthew reports an earthquake, the splitting of rocks, the opening of tombs, and the rising of many saints. Such phenomena are reminiscent of the Old Testament (Isaiah 26:19; Ezekial 37:12; Nahum 1:5–6). They represent the end of the old age and the start of the new. Not only the centurion makes a profession of faith, but the soldiers under his command as well (27:54). The gentiles also have access to the person and message of Jesus.

In Luke, the first words of Jesus on the cross are words of forgiveness for those responsible for his death (23:34; see Acts 3:17; 7:60). One of the two criminals condemned with Jesus rebukes his partner, acknowledges Jesus' innocence, and pleads for remembrance (23:40–42). Jesus assures this so-called good thief that he will be with him in paradise that very day (23:43). Instead of using Psalm 22 ("My God, my God, why have you forsaken me?") as in Matthew and Mark, Luke places Psalm 31:5 on Jesus' lips, prefaced by "Father": "...into your hands I commend my spirit" (23:46; see Acts 7:59). The centurion does not confess Jesus to be the Son of God. Rather, he proclaims Jesus' innocence (23:47). As a result of all these events, the Jewish crowd is moved to repentance (23:48: "beating their breasts"), a gesture recalling the humility of the tax collector in contrast to the haughty Pharisee (Luke 18:13).

While the Gospel of John has a great deal in common with the Synoptics, it also reveals unique perspectives. For example, Pilate confirms Jesus' kingship with a trilingual inscription (19:19–22). Paradoxically, the cross is his throne. Unlike Matthew and Mark, John explicitly cites Psalm 22:18 in the division of Jesus' clothes, emphasizing that Jesus' tunic was seamless and thereby perhaps viewing it as a symbol of unity (19:23–24). Whereas Matthew and Mark have the faithful women standing at a distance from the cross and make no mention of Jesus' male disciples, John places the witnesses at the foot of the cross, including the Mother of Jesus and the beloved disciple (19:25).

For John, both of these figures, while historical, have a key symbolic role here. While dying on the cross, Jesus designates (1) his own mother as the mother of the beloved disciple and (2) the beloved disciple as her son and hence the brother of Jesus (19:26–27). Now that Jesus' "hour" (19:27; see 2:4) has come, the Mother of Jesus makes her second and final appearance in this gospel. It is only appropriate that the Mother of Jesus be linked to the disciple whom Jesus loved.

The sponge soaked in wine is presented to Jesus on a sprig of hyssop (19:29). This alludes to the hyssop used to sprinkle the blood of the Passover lamb in Exodus 12:22. (Jesus' death sentence takes place at noon [19:14], the very time the priests started slaughtering the Passover lambs in the Temple.) Jesus' last words (19:30: "It is finished.") are a stark contrast to the cry of the distraught Jesus of Matthew and Mark. In this scene John anticipates Pentecost by having Jesus hand over the Spirit. In the blood and water flowing from the side of Jesus (19:34), John dramatizes the reality of Jesus' death (blood) and the gift of the Spirit (water). Since Jesus has now been glorified, the time has come to bestow the Spirit on Jesus' community (see John 7:38–39). The decision not to break Jesus' bones (19:33) is supported by a quote from Exodus 12:46 (19:36) that is yet another reference to the Passover lamb.

REFLECTIONS: We are not programmed to view Good Friday as Pentecost. We prefer to keep that Friday in a somber mood, one devoid of all joy and celebration. The Gospel of John tells us to do precisely the opposite. The death of Jesus is the birth of the Church because Jesus has communicated the Spirit to that body. The water flowing from the side of Jesus recalls Jesus' statement about himself as living water (John 7:37–38). Prior to Jesus' death, believers could not receive the Spirit because he was not yet glorified. On Calvary, Jesus entered into his glory and thus made possible the presence of the Spirit. Good Friday, therefore, is the occasion for joy, not sadness, for hallelujahs, not lamentations.

The Lukan Jesus must astound us as well. Usually when we are hurt, sick, or upset, we tend to concentrate on our own needs and problems, relegating to the most distant periphery the concerns of others. In this gospel, Jesus breaks this vicious cycle of the sole pursuit of self. The first words of the Lukan Jesus are words of forgiveness: "Father, forgive them; for they do not know what they are doing" (23:34). Obviously those responsible for his death come first; Jesus comes a distant second. In the episode with the so-called good thief, the Lukan Jesus reveals the capacity to listen to a distressed human being and to offer comfort and consolation. The Lukan Jesus teaches us to ask the right question. It is not: "What's in it for me?", but rather, "What's in it for you?" We discard our ego when we witness the needs of others and respond appropriately.

# CHAPTER FOUR

# THE GLORIOUS MYSTERIES

## The Resurrection

FOCUS: What does it mean to share the Word of God? In the Emmaus story, Jesus breaks open the Jewish Scriptures, expounds their meaning, and shows the link between suffering/death and glory/exaltation. It is hardly surprising that the hearts of the two Emmaus travelers were on fire. We share the Word of God when we research the text and try to uncover its original meaning. However, we also share that Word when we seek to learn what that Word means today. The text has a life of its own. To share the resurrection accounts is to accentuate the experience of the transformed Jesus. Jesus has conquered death, and in that act, he challenges us to be agents of transformation in the lives of others. In that sense, the empty tomb does mean a full life.

We become so used to the term "apostle" that we feel it

only applies to men. The Gospel of John, however, depicts Mary Magdalene, not only as one who experienced the risen Lord, but also as one who communicated that Good News to others. As we ponder the resurrection accounts, we see that the women are central to this great mystery. The women at the tomb proclaim the core reality of the event, that death has been swallowed up in victory.

TEXTS: Luke 24:1–53; John 20:1–29; see also Matthew 28:1–10; Mark 16:1–20; 1 Corinthians 15:3–8

TEXTUAL EXPLANATION: The resurrection is that unique act by which God raised and transformed forever the person Jesus (see Galatians 1:1). It is not a question of revivification or resuscitation (being brought back to life and expected to die again), as in the case of Lazarus. Through his resurrection, Jesus conquers death and returns immortal in power and glory. It is worth noting that we are not saved merely by the death of Jesus. Rather, the passion, death, resurrection, and ascension comprise one indissoluble action for our salvation (see Romans 4:25). The resurrection of Jesus expresses in a symbolic and metaphorical way our hope beyond death. To be sure, it is the same Jesus who becomes a life-giving spirit in the resurrection (1 Corinthians 15:45). However, there is obviously an element of change (Mark 16:12: "in another form"; see also John 20:14; 21:4). Not surprisingly, there is a whole gamut of reactions to this transformed Jesus, ranging from spontaneous faith to hostility.

In the body of the Emmaus story (24:16–31), Luke

dwells on two elements: (1) a dialogue narrative (24:17–27) and (2) a meal narrative (24:28–30). The dialogue first notes the travelers' acceptance of Jesus, but observes that the acceptance ended in tragedy (24:19–20). Next (24:21) the two travelers give expression to their personal hopes. And finally (24:22–23) they mention the report of the women at the tomb. Jesus responds (24:25–27) by expounding the Scriptures, especially the connection between tragedy and glory. In the meal narrative, the guest performs the tasks of the host. The language of blessing, breaking, and distributing has Eucharistic overtones. For Luke's audience, Jesus is both guest and host at the Christian meal. Luke suggests that those who share with others can rediscover the risen Lord and thus regain lost hope.

In John 20:1, Mary Magdalene is the first to arrive at the tomb, perhaps accompanied by other women. When she finds the tomb empty, she runs to tell Simon Peter and the beloved disciple. However, after the two male disciples have left the tomb, John remarks that Mary stayed outside crying (20:11). She next bends over into the tomb and finds two angels there who ask her about the reason for her weeping (20:13). Jesus then appears on the scene, although she does not recognize him at first, believing him to be the gardener (20:14–15). When Jesus pronounces her name, she responds by identifying him as Rabbouni/Teacher (20:16). According to John 10:4, sheep/followers recognize the shepherd when he calls them by name. Mary is without doubt a disciple of Jesus, since the name pronounced by the would-be gardener immediately leads to recognition of Jesus. At this point Jesus commissions Mary to take the news of the resurrection to the other disciples (20:17). Mary discharges her mission, announcing to the disciples: "I have seen the Lord" (20:18). By so doing, Mary functions as an apostle in that she reports Jesus' exaltation to his sisters and brothers.

**REFLECTIONS:** Jesus had not met the expectations of the two Emmaus travelers. For them the disaster of Good Friday had dashed all their hopes. They had resisted the report of the women about Jesus' resurrection. But Jesus then begins to break open the Scriptures for them so that they grasp the connection between suffering and death, on the one hand, and exaltation, on the other. Their reaction is poignantly noted is this passage: "Were not our hearts burning within us while he was talking to us on the road, while he was opening the scriptures to us?" (Luke 24:32).

The challenge, therefore, is to share the Word of God. We surely perform this task whenever we examine the Scriptures and indicate what the original author probably wanted to say. However, we also share the Word of God when we attempt to communicate what it means today. For example, we can reasonably conclude that Luke's passage means offering hospitality to strangers in our community. Yet hospitality can include more than a meal. It can also include providing hope and consolation for the depressed and the frustrated. It can extend to reaching deeper into our wallets and pocketbooks to feed the hungry and clothe

the naked. Whenever one despairing human being can see light at the end of the tunnel, then the Good News of the stranger on the Emmaus road is broken open and the risen One is again in our midst.

In the gospels, women play a significant role in announcing the resurrection of Jesus. Conspicuous among these women is Mary Magdalene. According to Matthew 28:8 and John 20:18, she functions as an apostle. She is the one who encounters the risen Lord and then shares that encounter with others. In western Christian tradition, Mary Magdalene bears the title "apostola apostolorum," the female apostle to the male apostles. As we ponder this scene in John, we must envision the contemporary apostolic roles of women. Their gospel message must become contagious so that the community can benefit from their talents and gifts. The Christian community is called to reflect the attitude of the historical Jesus toward women as well as that of Saint Paul (see Romans 16). Latter-day Mary Magdalenes should be alive and well among us, since the reality of the risen Lord comes upon us, in part at least, through their witness and message.

## The Ascension

FOCUS: The scene of Jesus' ascension in Acts 1 invites us to become involved in the mission of the Church. The two men in white robes address the same question to us: "... why do you stand looking up toward heaven?" (Acts 1:11). Through our baptism we become not onlookers, but vital participants in the life of the Church. To celebrate the ascension is to acknowledge our sense of mission.

As part of the larger mystery running from the passion to Pentecost, the ascension represents our hope beyond death. The Jesus who now enjoys the presence of the Father at his right hand embodies that hope. Death is not the end, but only a beginning. "Where, O death, is your victory? Where, O death, is your sting?" (1 Corinthians 15:55). The ascension powerfully reminds us that our ultimate destiny is to share in the glory of the risen Lord in the company of all the faithful.

TEXTS: Acts 1:3–11; see also Mark 16:19; Luke 24:51; John 20:17; Ephesians 4:10; 1 Timothy 3:16; Hebrews 4:14; 1 Peter 3:21–22

TEXTUAL EXPLANATION: For most Christians, the ascension evokes the scene of Jesus' being lifted up to heaven on a cloud forty days after Easter. However, the number forty is symbolic and cannot always be pressed mathematically. In fact, in other passages (Mark 16:19; Luke 24:51; John 20:17), Jesus ascends to the Father on Easter itself. The following distinction may add some clarity to the complexity of the traditions. Considered as the conclusion of the appearances of the risen Lord, the ascension occurred sometime after Jesus' resurrection, perhaps figuratively described as being raised up. Considered theologically as Jesus' return to the Father or his glorification at the right hand of God, the ascension forms an essential component of the resurrection of Jesus. Thus, after being glorified in his resurrection, Jesus appears as one endowed with supreme power (Matthew 28:18; Luke 24:26). In this way the ascension seeks to depict the complex phase of Jesus' existence that we speak of as his resurrection, glorification, or passage to the Father, together with his ongoing presence to the Church through the Spirit. This complex phase, including the death of Jesus, is properly called the paschal (Passover) mystery.

The passage in Acts 1 is programmatic for the theology of Luke. He shows the link between Jesus and the new community by insisting on Jesus' teaching after the resurrection. "Forty days" is used in rabbinic writings to show that the teaching of the disciple is authentic and authoritative, i.e., after such a period he is able to repeat the master's teaching. Jerusalem is to be the scene of the reception of the Spirit (1:4–5). Verse 6 is a reply to those who expected an imminent second coming of Jesus. It is a question of getting on with the work of the community and disregarding any timetable. Verse 8 describes the missionary endeavors of the new community: Jerusalem, Samaria, and the end of the earth. On the basis of Isaiah 49:6 and Acts 13:46–47, "the end of the earth" refers to the gentile mission.

Luke is the only author who speaks of two different ascensions. In Luke 24:51, Jesus is taken up into heaven on the day of the resurrection itself; this looks to Jesus' exaltation at the right hand of the Father. However, the ascension in Acts 1 focuses on the mission of the Church by interpreting Jesus' departure in terms of promoting the future of this new community. After Jesus' appearances, the Church is now to settle down to its normal life. However, it is still connected to Jesus because of the presence of the Spirit.

**REFLECTIONS:** The scene in Acts speaks to our involvement in the Church. Like the disciples, we are not to be standing around looking up at the sky. All of us are intended to be active participants playing a key role in the Spirit-filled community of Jesus. Such participation stems from our baptism, whereby we are constituted kings/queens, priests, and prophets. We possess a royal dignity because we are members of Jesus' extended family. We perform priestly functions, for example, actively sharing in the celebration of the Eucharist. We have a prophetic office, since Jesus empowers us to address the needs of the Church, whether for weal or woe. To that extent, the ascension is a demanding call to live out the implications of our baptism.

Considering the ascension as an indispensable component in the complex of death-resurrection-return to the Father-bestowal of the Spirit, we can readily understand why Good Friday was not God's last word. It was not all a tragic mistake, a quirk of fate, the end of what might have been. Death became the condition for birth into glory as the Father raised Jesus, transformed and empowered him, and ushered him into his presence at his right hand. This ascension experience of Jesus provides a basis for our own hope beyond death. We too long to make the same journey in which death will be swallowed up in victory (see 1 Corinthians 15:54–55). To that degree, the ascension empowers and energizes us as we continue, full of hope, to our final goal in the company of our extended family.

## The Descent of the Spirit

FOCUS: Unity, not division, is the work of the Spirit. In Acts 2 we learn that Pentecost is nothing less than the reversal of the Tower of Babel. The passage challenges us to think of Pentecost as an ongoing reality. We become the Spirit's agents by helping to transform hatred into love and enmity into reconciliation.

We also learn from the Gospel of John that the Paraclete performs a variety of functions, for example, teaching and consoling. However, if the Paraclete is to carry out these tasks, we must be involved. We too are called upon to breathe the Spirit in this fragile world of ours. We are to be latter-day paracletes.

TEXTS: John 14:15–17, 25–26; 15:18–27; 16:5–15; Acts 2:1–13; see also Acts 4:23–31; 8:14–17; 10:44–49

TEXTUAL EXPLANATION: Luke begins his account of Pentecost by linking the event with the fulfillment of Jesus' promise in Luke 24:49 and Acts 1:4–5, namely, to send the Spirit. Pentecost was an agricultural feast but was later identified with the giving of the Law on Sinai. For Luke, Pentecost means the start of a mission to the whole world that obliterates every human division and has the Spirit as its driving force.

The fire and the great sound are related to the covenant-making on Sinai (Exodus 19:16, 18). The international list of Jews and proselytes (gentile converts to Judaism who accepted circumcision), as well as the use of "confused" and "parted," connect Pentecost with the Tower of Babel (Genesis 11:7, 9; Deuteronomy 32:8). But here the outcome is vastly different: unity, not confusion, ensues. The remark in verse 13 that the disciples were filled with new wine suggests an original background of speaking in tongues. Quite likely Luke has transformed such frenzied speech into a speaking in other tongues or languages. It is this gift of the Spirit that inaugurates the Church, impelling the community to begin preaching the word.

In the Gospel of John, the term "paraclete" has several different layers of meaning that correspond to the needs of the Christian community, as the time lengthened between the departure of Jesus and his Second Coming. A first meaning of paraclete is *consoler*. In John 14:16, Jesus promises to give the disciples another paraclete (also known as "Advocate"). Jesus is the first Paraclete, and the Spirit is the second who continues Jesus' work. Moreover, the Spirit will be not only *with* the disciples but also *within* them (John 14:17) to strengthen their faith and console them in dealing with ever new problems. A second meaning of paraclete is *teacher* or *guide*. In John 14:26, the Paraclete will teach the disciples everything and remind them of all that Jesus taught. Thus the revelation begun by Jesus does not suddenly stop. The Paraclete unfolds the full significance of Jesus' words. As guide, the Paraclete will act in conformity with Jesus' teaching but will go beyond it (John 16:13). In this way, the Paraclete will develop the message of Jesus.

A third meaning of paraclete is *witness*. The disciples will experience the world's hatred just as Jesus did. In John this hatred takes the form of rejecting Jesus and his message. However, the Paraclete comes to the aid of the beleaguered disciples by bearing witness to Jesus. The Paraclete acknowledges the success of Jesus' mission and role, thereby urging the disciples to bear their own witness to the scandal of the cross (John 15:26–27). A fourth meaning of paraclete is *lawyer*. In John 16:8, the Paraclete acts as a prosecuting attorney. He thus proves the opposition to be wrong and Jesus to be right. By exposing the real criminal (the devil, the ruler of this world), the real nature of the crime (the rejection of Jesus), and Jesus' vindication (John 16:9–11), the Paraclete assures the disciples that they too can withstand the crisis and renew themselves.

REFLECTIONS: In Luke's account of the first Christian Pentecost, we most likely see the reversal of the Tower of Babel episode. According to Genesis 11:1–9, the hubris of humans who originally spoke only one language gave way to confusion. The plurality of languages meant their dispersion over the face of the entire earth. Instead of unity, there was division. For Luke, Pentecost is the precise opposite of the Tower of Babel. The one language (Aramaic) is now understood by an international host of non-Aramaic speakers. Instead of division, there is unity grounded in the driving force of the Spirit.

This sense of Pentecost challenges us to be the agents of unity and hence reconciliation. Division takes a variety of forms: domestic, ecclesial, international, and so on. Our first effort, it seems, must be in our homes and communities. By enabling estranged family members to begin speaking to one another, we are agents of the Spirit. By trying to settle differences and dichotomies in our own local communities, including in our parishes, we are participants in the ongoing celebration of Pentecost. We must celebrate Pentecost daily, not just once a year (see Acts 4:23–31; 8:14–17; 10:44–49).

The various roles of the Paraclete in the Gospel of John must be central in our lives. Unlike the earthly Jesus, the Paraclete, our bridge between Jesus and the Church, is invisible. If the Paraclete is to console, teach, guide, witness, and prosecute, only those within whom the Paraclete resides can perform these ministries. We are not called upon to exercise all these ministries. Rather, we are invited to examine our particular gifts and discover which ministry or ministries we can undertake. In so doing, we unleash the Spirit to make Pentecost an ongoing reality. The Paraclete and Spirit-filled believers go hand in glove.

## The Assumption of Mary

FOCUS: All too often the mystery of the assumption may create a sense of awe by which we divorce the Mother of Jesus from our world. We may tend (implicitly at least) to disassociate ourselves from Mary since she is in a class by herself, totally removed from our "real" situations. This mystery, however, actually brings us closer to the family bond we share with Mary and her Son. In her assumption, she is associated with Jesus and his extended family. The assumption implies that she shares in her Son's resurrection. Like him, she has participated in that transforming process by which we are finally and completely redeemed. In this way Mary embodies our hope of final salvation, not only in soul, but also in body. By sharing in the resurrection experience of Jesus, who is both the first fruits and the firstborn of the dead, she symbolizes hope for all of us.

TEXT: 1 Corinthians 15:35–49

TEXTUAL EXPLANATION: According to Pius XII's apostolic constitution (*Munificentissimus Deus*, 1950), Mary, having completed the course of her earthly life, was assumed body and soul to eternal glory. This document does not settle the question of whether Mary died at all. It also says nothing about the manner and time of her assumption. A positive element in this dogma is that believers have a destiny for glory, not only in the spiritual realm, but also in the physical one. To that extend the assumption of Mary is clearly a sign of human hope. The Church perceives in her assumption its own model and its own future in the resurrection of the body.

The idea of Mary's assumption is linked to her having stood in God's presence, for example, in the annunciation scene where she receives God's message from the angel and experiences the overshadowing of the power of the Most

High. Her role as an intercessor has some basis in the wedding feast of Cana (John 2:5) and is somewhat reminiscent of the intercessory roles of Moses (Exodus 32:11–14), Samuel (Jeremiah 15:1), and Jeremiah (Jeremiah 15:11). Her association with the disciples of Jesus is also seen in her presence on Calvary (John 19:25–27) and her prayerful participation with the Eleven, some women, and the brothers of Jesus prior to Pentecost (Acts 1:14). Although there is no clear biblical evidence for Mary's assumption, there is an approach for appreciating that doctrine in light of Paul's understanding of the resurrection of the body.

Some in Paul's Corinthian community held that the body was morally irrelevant. For such Christians, all that mattered was the soul. They concluded that, since the body is inconsequential in this life, it seems to make no sense to raise it after death. In this section of First Corinthians, Paul sets out to demonstrate the centrality of the body. To deny such centrality is to deny the incarnational dimension of the Christian message.

In this section of his letter, Paul elaborates on the character of the resurrected body by relating it to the resurrected body of Jesus. Paul begins by commenting on plant life. The plant that emerges from the seed is the same reality, but it possesses a fundamentally different body. It is God who determines the final form of the plant body. However, no one could divine his intention from the form of the seed body, especially since so many seeds are very similar.

Paul advances his argument by showing that the terms "flesh," "body," and "glory" do not have the same meaning when they are applied to the many diverse forms of "flesh," "body," and "glory." For example, "flesh" when predicated of a human being is vastly different from that of an animal. Having made this observation, Paul moves on to speak of the resurrected body. He does so by contrasting "before" (present body) and "after" (resurrected body). While the present body is perishable, dishonorable, weak, and physical, the resurrected body is imperishable, glorious, powerful, and spiritual. All who are in Christ (2 Corinthians 3:18) possess such "glory" in an incipient way, but they will enjoy it completely in their resurrected body.

To make his perception of such a resurrected body more concrete, Paul appeals to the experience of Jesus. He speaks of the first Adam in Genesis 1:1—2:25 as physical/natural, but then contrasts this Adam with the last Adam, namely, Christ. For Paul this last Adam is humanity as God initially intended humanity to be. Whereas the first Adam became a living being, the last Adam became a life-giving Spirit. Paul concludes by noting that, just as we have borne the image of the earthly Adam, we shall also bear the image of the heavenly Adam. In other words, we shall possess a resurrected body like that of Christ.

REFLECTIONS: All too often we think of the assumption as a purely personal privilege for Mary. We tend to separate her from Jesus and his sisters and brothers. However, according to Paul, the assumption of Mary would have to be rooted in the resurrection experience of Jesus himself. Paul speaks of Jesus as "the first fruits of those who have died"

(1 Corinthians 15:20). The image of first fruits suggests the consecration of the entire harvest. Hence Jesus' resurrection embraces all believers. The author of Colossians describes Jesus as "the firstborn from the dead" (Colossians 1:18). By this expression the author understands Jesus to be the zenith of the whole new order of creation. In brief, Jesus' resurrection is the model and exemplar for all believers.

Against this background we must envision Mary as fully sharing in the transformation process of her Son. In her assumption Mary is associated not only with Jesus, but also with us, his extended family. As she was associated during her lifetime with the family of Jesus' disciples, she remains connected to us as the paragon of hope. In her assumption she expresses the destiny of the believing community. Far from being a purely personal privilege, the assumption is the communal treasure of the Church.

Too frequently we tend to picture heaven on the last day as the pearly white enclave of disembodied spirits. The assumption, however, reminds us in a most powerful way that the glory of the resurrected body of Jesus impacts our bodies as well. Hence on the last day, heaven is not just a gathering place for souls. Another way of saying this is that the assumption demonstrates the dignity of the human body. Our bodies that are washed in baptism, nourished in the Eucharist, and strengthened in confirmation are destined to experience the transformation of Jesus' resurrected body. The assumption affected not only Mary's soul but also her body. As such, she radiates in her total person (body and soul) the glory of "the firstborn of the dead"

(Colossians 1:18). To honor Mary in her assumption is to anticipate our final destiny, one grounded in him who is "the first fruits of those who have died" (1 Corinthians 15:20).

# The Coronation of Mary as Queen of Heaven and Earth

FOCUS: To speak of Mary's coronation as the queen of heaven and earth is to announce her involvement with all the sisters and brothers of Jesus. In Revelation 12, she is linked to her offspring who continue to endure the wiles of the dragon. Where Mary is, there is also the extended family of her Son. To honor Mary as queen is to recognize her benevolent role of protecting and safeguarding this family. This queen adamantly refuses to be isolated from the ongoing needs and concerns of her Son's sisters and brothers.

This passage in Revelation reminds us to look beyond the Roman Empire and its dangers to our own situation. Like the audience of Revelation, we too are prone to a society that lusts after power and prestige. The seer of Revelation urges us to reject all the societal values that are opposed to the gospel. In the final analysis, we have to choose our loyalties and priorities.

TEXT: Revelation 12:1–17

TEXTUAL EXPLANATION: The Book of Revelation falls under the genre of apocalyptic. It is a form of revelatory literature set within a narrative framework in which an otherworldly being communicates a revelation to a human recipient. In this case Jesus reveals the message to an angel who, in turn, shares it with John. Typical of such literature is a very generous use of symbolic images. Such literature also focuses on times of crisis. Here the crisis is the Roman Empire, especially with its imperial cult, during the time of Domitian (81–96 AD). For the author, the value system of the Roman Empire is "public enemy number one," in that it seeks to entice Christians away from the value system of Jesus. This work is fundamentally a vision of hope, since victory was actually won on the cross. The task of Christians, therefore, is to persevere in their faith commitment.

In Revelation 12:1–17, there are three sections in the narrative. The first (12:1–6) takes place in heaven and involves the woman, the dragon, and the woman's child. The second (12:7–12) starts in heaven, but eventually comes down to earth with Michael and the dragon as antagonists. The third (12:13–17) is set on earth and involves the dragon, the woman, and the woman's offspring.

Who is the woman in the account? The most plausible identification is that she personifies Israel, the people of God in the Old Testament. However, in its Christian form, she is the Church, the New Testament people of God.

The birth of the Messiah is not to be localized in Bethlehem. Rather, the birth suggests the dawning of messianic salvation. The taking of the child to God and his throne does not imply Jesus' resurrection or ascension. Instead, that event underlines the protection of this Messiah. Though the dragon has been defeated in heaven, the battle still rages on earth. Hence the scene urges ongoing perseverance on the part of the woman's offspring on earth.

While the primary Christian reference to the woman in this account is the Church, namely, the people of God in the Christian Scriptures, a secondary reference to Mary, the Mother of Jesus, remains a distinct possibility. Such a possibility arises from the eventual inclusion of the Book of Revelation in the New Testament canon. When the images of Mary in Luke/Acts and the Gospel of John are read alongside the image of the woman in Revelation 12, it is at least conceivable that such images could reinforce each other.

**REFLECTIONS:** It is of the utmost importance that Mary be viewed in the context of the entire people of God. This scene in Revelation captures the significance of the woman in the setting of her offspring who continue to endure the wiles of the dragon. To speak of the coronation of Mary and her queenship is to conceive of this woman as utterly and intrinsically connected to the sisters and brothers of Jesus. This mystery assures us that we are all joined together. Heaven is never single file. Rather, it is the image of an extended family whose members draw strength from each other. Where Mary is, there also are the sisters and brothers of Jesus.

Although other biblical authors paint the picture of civil government in more positive colors (see Romans 13:1–7; 1 Peter 2:13–17), the author of Revelation sees nothing but evil in the Roman Empire. Such an institution is the implacable enemy of the followers of Jesus, because its value system runs counter to that of the Gospel. Such an attitude may well give us pause. Daily we are exposed to the gospel of American values that often smacks of the primacy of power, prestige, and wealth. The seer of Revelation challenges us to examine the underlying principles of this gospel and to discover those areas where that gospel and the gospel of Jesus are in conflict. This does not entail flight from the world. Rather, it is a challenge to determine where our final allegiance lies. To that extent, the message of Revelation is as timely as ever.